Arduino for the

Arduino for the Cloud

Arduino Yún and Dragino Yún Shield

Claus Kühnel

Universal-Publishers
Boca Raton

Arduino for the Cloud: Arduino Yún and Dragino Yún Shield

Universal-Publishers
Boca Raton, Florida • USA
2015

ISBN-10: 1-62734-035-1
ISBN-13: 978-1-62734-035-9

www.universal-publishers.com

The Linux Penguin is a work of authors
Larry Ewing, Simon Budig and Anja Gerwinski.

Arduino Yun photo by Dog Hunter LLC.

Dragino photo by WangHui.

This book and the circuits described, procedures and programs have
been carefully created and tested. Nevertheless, errors and
mistakes cannot be excluded.

Preface

Raspberry Pi and comparable computer modules use embedded Linux as an operating system with the result that embedded Linux is no longer reserved for specialists alone, but can be used by amateurs and enthusiasts as well. At the same time, a way has been opened to start with a class of completely new tasks. The base for communication among several components has been laid and we are able to develop the Internet of Things (IoT).

Wikipedia provides a comprehensive description of the IoT. Embedded systems with limited resources can collect data from natural ecosystems as well as from buildings and factories. Otherwise, these systems could also be responsible for performing actions like ordering missing goods in a storage system. Energy management and transport optimization, as heard of these days at the Port of Hamburg, are further examples.

In the paper entitled "The Computer for the 21st Century" [1], Mark Weiser (http://en.wikipedia.org/wiki/Mark_Weiser) spoke about this vision for the first time in 1991.

Today, the Arduino family comprises more than 20 boards (not including Arduino clones) and creates a largely mature platform for building professional prototypes. The unusual concept of open-source hardware and software was awarded the Prix Ars Electronica in Linz in 2006.

If we look into the relevant forums and portals covering microcontroller technology, we cannot miss the topic of Arduino.

Google provided a further impulse through its decision to use Arduino as the Android Open Accessory kit [2]. Arduino is an open-source prototyping platform based on flexible and easy-to-use hardware and software.

The primary goal for using Arduino is direct contact with the environment. Arduino can detect signals from sensors and control this environment via several actors. The term "physical computing" describes the kind of applications for which access to the environment is an important attribute.

The high complexity of today's requirements for electronic systems cannot be implemented by concepts based on classic microcontrollers. In most cases, the networking of components is indispensable. In the absence of these preconditions, the IoT would be wishful thinking.

Arduino Yún combines the classic Arduino based on Atmel's AVR microcontrollers with an Atheros AR9331 System-on-a-Chip (SoC). This SOC is used in WLAN access points and routers, and runs the Linux distribution Linino (OpenWRT) as operating system.

The family of Arduino shields has recently been extended by Dragino's Yún shield. The combination of the Dragino Yún shield with an Arduino Leonardo can be compared with an Arduino Yún.

While an Arduino Leonardo with the Dragino Yún shield together is functionally identical to Arduino Yún, the Yún shield offers more flexibility through possible combinations with Arduino Uno, Duemilanove, Mega, etc. In addition, the Dragino Yun shield uses an external WiFi antenna that promises more stability and robustness of the wireless connection.

The operating system Linino (OpenWRT) offers interface drivers, a file system and multi-threading, among other things, and is responsible for recurring tasks using stable software components.

This book is a translation of "Arduino für die Cloud" (ISBN 978-3-907857-25-0), which was published in German. It deals with the Arduino Yun and the combination of Arduino Leonardo with the Dragino Yun shield and considers both implemented controllers and their interaction.

All listed sources and some explanations can be found at SourceForge under http://sourceforge.net/projects/arduinoynsnippets/.

For ease of readability, I follow in the textual representation the conventions listed below:

- Commands and output to the console are represented in Courier New.
- Inputs via console are in **Courier New**.
- Program and file names appear in *Italian.*

All existing links were checked in the autumn of 2014. As the internet changes continuously, it cannot be assured that these links will work or lead to the same content as at the time of admission. Please inform me about broken links.

Altendorf, spring 2015
Claus Kühnel

Content

1 Introduction

If you want to extend an Arduino so that it is network enabled, then you could use, for example, an Arduino Uno supplemented with an Ethernet shield or you could use an Arduino Ethernet. The Ethernet shield and the Arduino Ethernet provide an Ethernet interface based on the WIZnet Hardwired TCP/IP Embedded Ethernet Controller W5100.

Figure 1 shows an Ethernet shield that can be placed on an Arduino and provides them an Ethernet interface.

Figure 2 shows an Arduino Ethernet, a combination of an Arduino and an Ethernet interface on one board. The difference from other Arduino boards is the missing USB-to-serial chip. The Ethernet part is identical to the Ethernet shield.

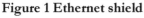

Figure 1 Ethernet shield　　　　**Figure 2 Arduino Ethernet**

The Arduino Yún differs from other Arduino boards through its capabilities to communicate with the Linux system running on the Atheros AR9331. These capabilities make the Arduino Yún a powerful platform for Linux application in a network and IoT projects combined with the simplicity of the Arduino. Additionally to powerful Linux commands like *cURL*, an option is to use one's own Shell or Python scripts for a robust interaction with Arduino Yún.

The Arduino Yún is similar to the Arduino Leonardo because Arduino Leonardo uses an ATmega32u4 too. Since the ATmega32u4 has an integrated USB controller, it has no need for a second controller, like an FT232 for example. The Arduino Yún represents itself against a connected computer additionally to the virtual (communication device class) COM port as mouse, keyboard or another HID interface.

Figure 3 shows the front side of an Arduino Yún. In the upper part, you can see the Atheros AR9331, a 2.4 GHz System-on-a-Chip (SoC) developed for WLAN and router applications.

Figure 4 shows the rear of an Arduino Yún with an AU6350 Single-Chip-USB 2.0 hub and multimedia card reader controller and an SD card holder.

On the rear, you can see the internationality of this product. The fathers of the Arduino are from Italy. Dog Hunter, which is located in the U.S.A., developed the board. The layout work was done in Switzerland and production in Taiwan.

Figure 3
Arduino Yún—front view

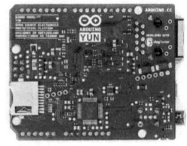

Figure 4
Arduino Yún—rear view

Launched by the Chinese company Dragino (http://www.dragino.com), the Dragino Yún shield includes all the components of the Arduino Yun without the ATmega32u4. The Dragino Yún shield gets the Arduino Yún functionality by connecting it to an Arduino Leonardo. But it is possible to connect alternative Arduino boards with the Dragino Yún shield, too.

The encapsulated Dragino HE Module is the core of the Dragino Yún shield. Its Atheros AR9331 SoC runs the same Linino (OpenWRT) as Linux distribution, as for Arduino Yún. Figure 5 shows the top view of the Dragino Yun shield.

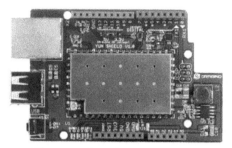

Figure 5 Dragino Yún shield

This book explains the start-up of the Arduino Yún and the Dragino Yún shield connected to an Arduino Leonardo and their use. These explanations should provide a quick overview of the enhanced possibilities of these LAN- and WLAN-capable Arduinos.

Detail information about the Arduino Yún and the Dragino Yún shield can be found via the following URLs:

- http://arduino.cc/en/Main/ArduinoBoardYun
- http://www.dragino.com/products/yunshield/item/86-yun-shield.html

2 Arduino Yún

This chapter describes the similarities and differences between the Arduino Yún and the Dragino Yún shield. Hence, possible hurdles are largely eliminated when using one of the two platforms.

2.1 Power Supply

2.1.1 Arduino Yún

The micro-USB interface is a common way to connect an Arduino with a power supply. Furthermore, this connection serves as a communication path to the Arduino development environment (IDE).

 The Arduino Yún has no voltage regulator onboard; therefore, the voltage at pin VIN has to be 5V DC constant. Pay attention to this requirement when choosing the power supply.

Another possibility is to source the Arduino Yún via the Ethernet. The board is prepared for the use of a Power over Ethernet (PoE) module.

Power supply details:

VIN	External connection for supply voltage of 5 V DC
5V	Internal 5 V supply voltage Voltage source can be VIN or USB
3V3	Internal 3.3 V supply voltage, generated by an on-board regulator. Load can be 50 mA
GND	Ground
IOREF	Voltage of the I/O pins (VCC = 5 V)

2.1.2 Dragino Yún Shield

The Dragino Yún shield gets its supply voltage from the connected Arduino board.

The Dragino HE draws under full load approximately 200 mA. Its supply voltage is derived from the voltage at VIN of the Arduino board and will be converted on the Dragino Yún shield itself to 3.3 V DC. The Dragino Yún shield should be powered under these conditions via a VIN voltage of the Arduino board between 7 and 15 V DC and not via the USB connection.

The supply voltage for the USB host is derived from +5 V DC of the Arduino. To avoid overheating of the voltage regulator on Arduino when using the USB host, the voltage at VIN should be limited to 7 V DC.

When using the Dragino Yun shield, I have always worked with a voltage of 7 V DC on pin VIN. The average current consumption was 0.15 A in this case.

2.2 Memory

2.2.1 Arduino Yún

The ATmega32u4 used on Arduino Yún has a 32 KB flash memory. The boot loader uses 4 KB of this memory. The ATmega32u4 provides 2.5 KB of RAM and 1 KB of EEPROM for use. The EEPROM library supports reading and writing of that EEPROM.

The Atheros AR9331 has no internal memory. On board is 64 MB of DDR2RAM and a 16 MB flash memory. The Linux distribution Linino (OpenWRT) is factory-installed in the flash memory. This factory image can be changed. A reset to the factory-installed image can be achieved by pressing the key WLAN RST for 30 seconds.

The existing memory can be enhanced by a micro-SD card or a USB memory stick. SD card and USB connectors are available on board.

2.2.2 Dragino Yún Shield

The Dragino Yún shield also has a 64 MB RAM and a 16 MB flash memory but the memory on the Arduino side is defined by the connected Arduino board.

I use here an Arduino Leonardo and the ATmega32u4 used on Arduino Leonardo provides 32 KB of flash memory once again (4 KB are occupied by the boot loader) as well as 2.5 KB RAM and 1 KB EEPROM. The EEPROM library supports reading and writing of the EEPROM again.

2.3 I/O

2.3.1 Arduino Yún I/O

All I/O pins on Arduino Yún that can be connected externally are pins of the ATmega32u4 microcontroller. The programming of these pins occurs Arduino-conform with the instructions `pinMode()`, `digitalWrite()` and `digitalRead()`.

All pins operate with 5 V (defined by IOREF) and can source or draw a current of 40 mA pro pin maximum. Pull-up resistors are available in a range between 20 and 50 kΩ, but these are disabled by default.

Several pins have alternative functions:

Function	Pin	Description
Serial	0 (RX) 1 (TX)	Receiving (RX) and transmitting (TX) serial data with TTL level from/to the ATmega32u4 hardware interface. The class **Serial** refers to the USB (CDC) interface. The class **Serial1** refers to the TTL communication to the AR9331 via pins 0 and 1.
TWI(I^2C)	2 (SDA) 3 (SCL)	I^2C interface The Wire library supports this communication.
External Interrupts	0 (INT2) 1 (INT3) 2 (INT1) 3 (INT0) 7 (INT4)	These pins can be used as interrupt lines. The pins can be configured to the following interrupt requests: Low at pin, rising or falling edge or change of the level. Details are described at function `attachInterrupt()`. Pins 0 and 1 should not be used as inter-

		rupt line, because these lines are used for serial communication between ATmega32u4 and AR9331. Pin 7 is connected to the AR9331 too and could be used as handshake line later. Therefore, only pins 2 and 3 are available for unscrupulous use as interrupt lines, if you do not use the I²C interface.
PWM	3, 5, 6, 9, 10, 11, 13	8-bit PWM output using the function `analogWrite()`.
SPI	ICSP Header	SPI data transfer using the SPI library. The SPI pins of Arduino Yún are connected to the ICSP header only. This can mean restrictions for the use of Arduino shields. The SPI pins are connected to the AR9331; hence, ATmega32u4 and AR9331 can transfer data via SPI too.
LED	13	This is the well-known internal LED connected to pin 13 onboard (Hi = LED on, Lo = LED off).
Analog Input	A0–A5, 4 (A6) 6 (A7) 8 (A8) 9 (A9) 10(A10) 12(A11)	Arduino Yún has 12 analog inputs (A0–A11) with a resolution of 10 bits. Per default, the input voltage range is 0–5 V. This range can be reduced by the use of the AREF pin and the function `analogReference()`.
AREF		Reference voltage for analog inputs. Usage with the function `analogReference()`.
Yún RST		A low level on this pin resets the AR9331. The Linux system will be rebooted. All data in the RAM are lost. Running programs will be stopped. Files can be corrupted.
32U4 RST		A low level on this pin resets the ATmega32u4.

WLANRST		The primary function is to reset WiFi to the factory setup. The factory setup is the Access Point Mode (AP) and the fix IP address 192.168.240.1. In this mode, the Arduino Yún can be configured. A reset of the WiFi configuration forces a reboot of the Linux system. To reset the WiFi configuration, press the key WLAN RST for five seconds. The secondary function is to reset the Linux system to the factory image. To reset the Linux system, press the key WLAN RST for 30 seconds. All data stored in the flash memory is lost.

Additionally, the Arduino Yún has some LEDs onboard:

Marking	Function
RX	Serial receiver
TX	Serial transmitter
L13	LED at IO13
WAN	WAN (Ethernet) indicator
ON	Power indicator
WLAN	WLAN (WiFi) indicator
USB	USB

2.3.2 Dragino Yún Shield I/O

The Dragino Yún shield does not make any I/O pins available outwards. In the combination of Arduino Board and the Dragino Yun shield, the available I/O pins come solely from the Arduino board.

Differences from the Arduino Yún:

S1:	S1 serves as reset key. Pressing it for five seconds resets the WiFi configuration. All other settings remain unchanged. Pressing it for 30 seconds resets the Linux system to the factory image.
SV1:	The jumper SV1 configures the voltage level for SPI and UART (5 V and 3.3 V respectively). Arduino Leonardo works with 5 V levels.

Additionally, the Dragino Yún shield has some LEDs onboard:

Marking	Function
PWR	Power indicator
LAN	LAN (Ethernet) indicator
WLAN	WLAN (WiFi) indicator
SYS	LED for USB memory. On = USB is connected to the Arduino Yun default SD directory /mnt/sd or /www/sd connected.

2.4 Communication

2.4.1 Arduino Yún

The Arduino Yún has several interfaces for communicating with a computer, another Arduino or another microcontroller.

The ATmega32u4 provides UART hardware with TTL levels for serial communication. This interface (IO0 and IO1) is used for serial communication between the ATmega32u4 and the Atheros AR9331. The Bridge library supports the software side.

In addition, the ATmega32u4 offers the possibility of serial communication over USB and is then viewed from a connected PC as a virtual COM port. The software download from the PC to the Arduino usually occurs through this interface equipped with a micro-USB connector. This interface can also be used for monitoring. The data transfer through this interface is indicated by the flashing of the RX and TX LEDs on the board.

Using the Software Serial Library, software UART's can be implemented, so that each pin of the ATmega32u4 can be used for serial communication. But IO0 and IO1 are reserved for the hardware UART. The ATmega32u4 supports I²C and SPI communication as well. The Wire library supports communication via the I²C bus and the SPI library that for the SPI bus.

Arduino Yún can be programmed as a generic keyboard and mouse. For this, keyboard and mouse classes are available.

The Atheros AR9331 provides the Ethernet and WiFi interfaces. The Bridge library is responsible for this communication too.

The Arduino Yún offers through Linux support, another USB host interface. Via this USB port, we can connect a memory stick for memory enhancement, a keyboard, a mouse, and a webcam. It may be necessary to install other software packages. I will return to this later.

2.4.2 Dragino Yún Shield

The Dragino HE module uses SPI and UART to communicate with the connected Arduino board. The Dragino Yún shield is compatible with 3.3 V and 5 V Arduino boards. The jumper SV1 on the Dragino Yún shield selects the used voltage level (3.3 V or 5 V).

The program upload from Arduino IDE uses the SPI interface and connects both controllers. SPI is free for other SPI slaves in an application program after this upload.

The UART interface (IO0 and IO1) serves as a bridge between both controllers as in Arduino Yún.

2.5 Initial Startup

The statements for the initial startup refer to the Arduino Yún and the combination of Arduino Leonardo—Dragino Yún Shield alike. I use here an Arduino Leonardo for the combination with the Dragino Yún shield, because it can be connected without additional modifications.

The steps required for connecting an Arduino Uno, Duemilanove/Diecimila as well as Mega2560 are described in detail in the Yun Shield User Manual—version 1.1; therefore, the link to the user manual, http://www.dragino.com/downloads/downloads/YunShield/YUN_SHIELD_USER_MANUAL_v1.0.pdf, seems sufficient here. In addition, the relevant boards are to be considered in the software configuration.

Before the initial startup of the Arduino Yún, the Arduino Development Environment must be downloaded from the Arduino website to the computer used for software development.

I use here a development PC running Microsoft Windows, for which you will find the installer at the URL http://downloads.arduino.cc/arduino-1.5.7-windows.exe. Installers for Linux and MacOS can be found in the same place.

Arduino 1.6.1 with several fixes and improvement for Arduino Yún also was released on 03/10/2015. Take this revision for new developments, although the program samples published here were tested using Arduino 1.5.7.

 The Arduino Yún is only supported as of version 1.5.4 of the development environment, which is important to remember before download.

Arduino enthusiasts, not unexpectedly, will get the known user interface to face. However, there is some news here. Figure 6 shows the list of supported Arduino boards, including our Arduino Yún at the top of the list.

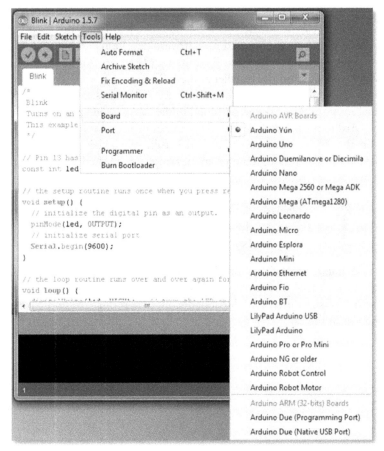

Figure 6 Arduino boards in the Tools menu

After connecting the micro-USB connector of the Arduino Yún with an USB port of your PC, the drivers install automatically and you can find the used COM port with the help of the device manager.

Figure 7 shows that our Arduino Yún is connected to the (virtual) port COM16 and it is possible to communicate via USB with the PC.

There is another interface named "myYUN at 192.168.1.29 (Arduino Yún)", which I will explain later.

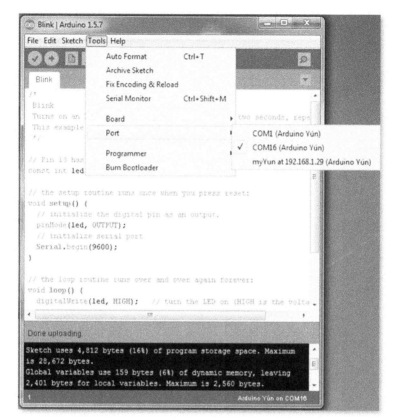

Figure 7 Arduino Yún communication interfaces

The Arduino program *blink.ino*, which may be inspected in the editor, can be uploaded via COM16 into the Arduino Yún.

This program provides a blinking red LED and periodic output of the character * via the USB port, which can be displayed in a monitor program (Figure 8). The baud rate of the monitor program must be equal to the baud rate defined in the function setup().

Figure 8 Monitor output

For those who already have experience in programming Arduino, these steps are not new. For the person who is using Arduino for the first time, the Arduino website http://arduino.cc offers good support.

There is also a lot of literature explaining Arduino now. Amazon.com shows 1,128 results for books with "Arduino" in the title. Please use your preferred search engine to find your solution.

As of Version 1.0 of the Arduino IDE, some changes have been introduced, which must be considered when porting programs from previous versions.

2.6 Architecture

On the Arduino Yun, two worlds meet. Figure 9 shows a block diagram of the Arduino Yún (http://arduino.cc/en/Main/ArduinoBoardYun).

On the left side, we see the Arduino based on an ATmega32u4 (http://www.atmel.com/devices/ATmega32u4.aspx) with a micro-USB connector for programming and communication with the Arduino IDE, which can be used to power the Arduino Yun simultaneously.

On the right side, we see the Linux device based on an Atheros AR9331 (http://www.datasheetspdf.com/PDF/AR9331/743003/24). The

Linux device is running Linino
(http://linino2013.wordpress.com/about/) derived from OpenWRT
(https://openwrt.org/).

With an Ethernet interface (eth1) and a wireless interface (wlan0), the Atheros AR9331 provides opportunities for integration into a network. In addition, an SD card interface and a USB host port are available for external expansion.

The Bridge library makes the communication between Atheros AR9331 and ATmega32u4 easier. We get the opportunity to run shell scripts, communicate with the network and obtain information from the AR9331 processor for an Arduino sketch out. The USB host as well as the network interface and the SD card are not connected to the ATmega32u4 but with the AR9331. The Bridge library also allows the ATmega32u4 to access the AR9331 periphery.

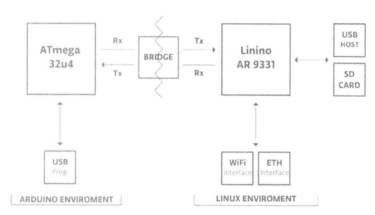

Figure 9 Arduino Yún block diagram

At Arduino Yún, the focus remains on the Arduino. However, Arduino enthusiasts get the opportunity to use web services over wired or wireless Ethernet, without deep knowledge of Linux. Due to the Atheros AR9331, which takes over the entire network management, the Linux side is encapsulated, but remains fully available. Some technical features of the Arduino Yún are summarized in Table 1. The part for the Atheros AR9331 applies to the Dragino Yún shield too, while the part for the ATmega32u4 applies for the Arduino Yún only. For the combination of Dragino Yún shield with an Arduino, the technical data of the used Arduino apply.

ATmega32u4	
Source voltage	5 V
Input voltage	5 V
Digital I/O	20
PWM outputs	7
Analog inputs	12
Current pro I/O pin	40mA
Current pro 3.3 V pin	50mA
Flash memory	32 KB (4 KB for Bootloader)
SRAM	2.5 KB
EEPROM	1 KB
Clock frequency	16 MHz
AtherosAR9331	
Architecture	MIPS@400MHz
Source voltage	3.3 V
Ethernet	IEEE802.310/100Mbit/s
WiFi	IEEE802.11b/g/n
USB type-A	2.0 Host/Device
Card reader	Micro-SD
RAM	64MB DDR2
Flash memory	16 MB

Table 1 Technical features of Arduino Yún

The structure of the Yún Shields can be understood by separating the Arduino Yún at the Bridge in Figure 9. Figure 10 shows the block diagram of the Dragino Yún shield.

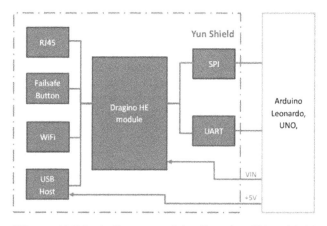

Figure 10 Block diagram of the Dragino Yún shield

The Arduino defined by the used Atmel AVR microcontroller is connected via SPI and UART with the Atheros AR9331 containing the Dragino HE module. The communication between the two controllers is the same as for the Arduino Yún on the Bridge library.

2.7 Arduino Yún in Network

Previously, a Windows or Linux PC with an Arduino development environment installed was required for software development for an Arduino. This Arduino had to be connected to that PC via USB for software upload. The necessary steps I have shown in Section 2.6.

With Arduino Yún or the combination of an Arduino board and the Dragino Yún shield, we now have a networkable controller and this has an impact on the development environment.

If there are no differences between Arduino Yún and the combination of the Arduino board—Dragino Yún shield, then I use the term Arduino Yún for both controllers. If there is a difference, then it will be mentioned explicitly.

To use the full functionality of both controllers, we integrate them into a network, as is certainly available in most homes.

I assume that the desktop PC is connected via Ethernet to a wireless router and, through this, to the internet. At this WLAN router, a network-attached storage (NAS, hard disk for backup) and, possibly, a printer are also (wired) connected. In addition, the wireless router is an access point (AP) for the different wireless devices, such as notebook, tablet or smartphone.

Figure 11 shows the integration of our Arduino into the described network. The Arduino is connected with the development PC via the on-board micro-USB connector. Via this connector, the Arduino obtains its power and the software upload occurs. Powering the Arduino–Dragino Yún shield combination differs and was described in Section 2.1.2 in detail. Overall, there is no difference with the classical approach.

Due to the presence of Ethernet and WLAN, we can integrate the Arduino Yún into the home network as well. I consider here primarily the wireless interface, because the Arduino Yún can be arranged without long cable connections near the sensors.

For powering the Arduino Yún, a mobile phone charger equipped with a micro USB connector can be used. For powering an Arduino with the Dragino Yún shield, we can use an AC adapter with the right connector to VIN and the right voltage. In Figure 11, this part is not shown.

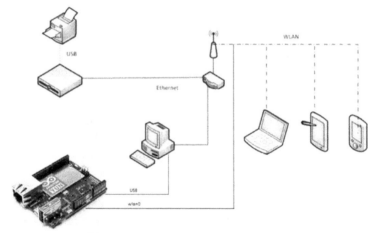

Figure 11 Arduino Yún in network

After a successful connection with Arduino Yún–XXXXXXXXXXXXX or Dragino 2–XXXXXXXXXXXXX the device is in the AP mode. A web browser can access the device via the URL http://arduino.local or 192.168.240.1.

I used for this my smartphone Galaxy S5 because my development PC is connected with the router by a wired connection. Any other WiFi-capable computer, tablet or phone can be used in this way.

After a short time, the Arduino Yún answers with its web interface. After the input of the default password "arduino", the web browser is connected to the web interface of the Arduino Yún.

Figure 12 shows the opening configuration window. I gave my Arduino Yún the name "myYún" and an eight-digit password. You need this later to gain access to your Arduino Yún.

After setting up the right time zone, you can select the network. I have selected WiFi only, input my SSID and the WPA2 password and that is all. After saving the configuration, a restart of the Arduino Yún occurs and it is connected to the home network (here, this is my D-Link router with SSID DSL-2740B; Figure 13).

Figure 12
WLAN configuration

Figure 13
WLAN restart

After completing the configuration, we can check our new network participant using a web browser. Figure 14 shows the access to an Arduino Yún with the URL 192.168.1.4, while Figure 15 shows the access to a Dragino Yún shield with the URL 192.168.1.25.

Figure 14 Web access to Arduino Yún

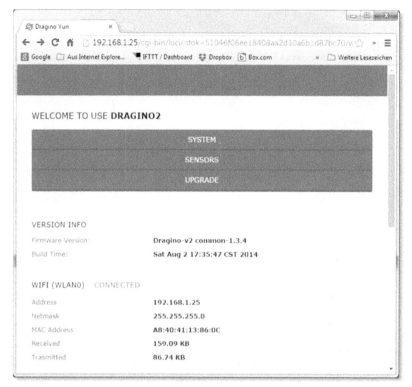

Figure 15 Web access to Dragino Yún shield

Since the Dragino Yún shield can work with different Arduino boards, there is a need for configuring the Bridge by pressing the button SENSORS.

Figure 16 shows the required input when an Arduino Leonardo is used as baseboard.

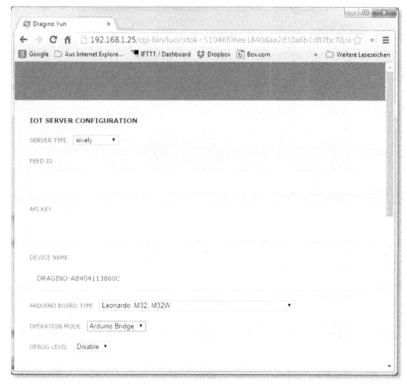

Figure 16 Bridge configuration

2.8 Firmware Upgrade

The firmware of the Arduino Yún and the Dragino Yún shield are subject to development. You can find the actual versions on the following locations for download:

- http://arduino.cc/en/Main/Software#toc8
- http://wiki.dragino.com/index.php?title=Yun_Firmware_Change_Log

I will show the firmware upgrade for the Dragino Yún shield as an example. Figure 17 shows the Firmware Change Log from Dragino Wiki. The actual version here was v1.3.5. Now you will find there v2.0.3. At delivery, my Dragino Yún shield had v1.3.4 installed.

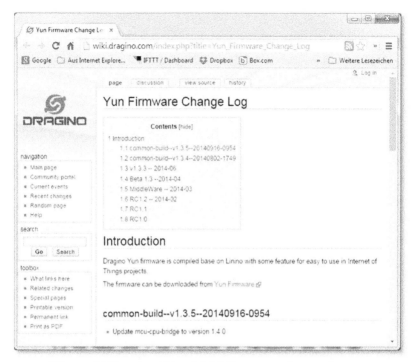

Figure 17 Dragino Yún shield firmware change log

We can find the available binaries for download at http://www.dragino.com/downloads/index.php?dir=motherboards/ms14/Firmware/Yun/. Interesting for us here is the file *dragino2-yun-common-v1.3.5-squashfs-sysupgrade.bin* (Figure 18).

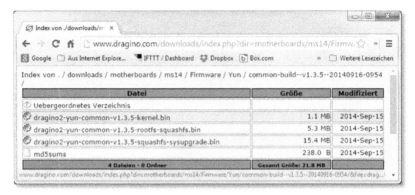

Figure 18 Available binaries

This file can be downloaded to the developer's PC and uploaded to the Dragino Yún shield afterward.

After a completed download, we can upgrade the Dragino Yún shield. By pressing the button PROCESS UPGRADE, the installation begins (Figure 19). Be patient, for this takes some time (Figure 20).

Figure 19 Firmware upload completed

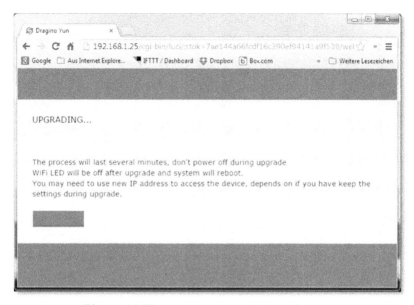

Figure 20 Firmware upgrade is running

3 Arduino Microcontroller

In this chapter, I present Arduino programs in a classical sketch format. At first, there are several programs without network connection but which are handled using the actual version of the Arduino IDE 1.5.7. Next, we look to programs that use the Bridge library for communication with the Atheros AR9331.

The combination of the functions presented leads to the solution of problems we know from everyday life.

3.1 Classical Arduino Development

In the standalone Arduino programs using the latest Arduino IDE 1.5.7, innovations must also be considered.

Since November 2011, the Arduino IDE Version 1.0 is already available. Some changes have been introduced than must be taken into account, especially when porting older Arduino programs.

 The file extension .pde previously used was changed to .ino to ensure the clear demarcation of processing files. Old .pde files are opened by IDEs from version 1.0, but then saved as .ino file. The reverse does not work.

Many Arduino libraries were written for IDE versions before 1.0. These libraries use other linked libraries if required.

After IDE version 1.0, *wiring.h*, *WProgram.h*, *WConstants.h* and *pins_arduino.h* were combined in *Arduino.h*.

Thus, it is advisable to write the following code in the libraries:

```
#if ARDUINO >= 100
#include "Arduino.h"
#else
#include "WProgram.h"
#endif
```

These notes should suffice here. More details about porting can be found in [3], for example. In addition to the changes in the IDE, there are also hardware-based changes through the use of ATmega32u4 against the ATmega328.

Figure 21 shows the pin out of the Arduino Yún (http://pighixxx.com/yunpdf.pdf) and Figure 22 that of Arduino Leonardo (http://pighixxx.com/leonardopdf.pdf). For better readability, download the PDFs in question via the links mentioned above.

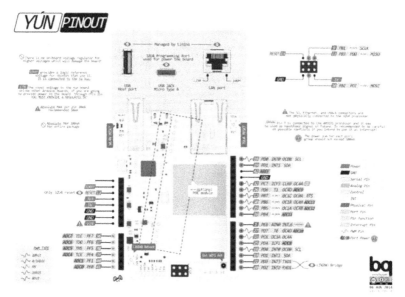

Figure 21 Pin out Arduino Yún

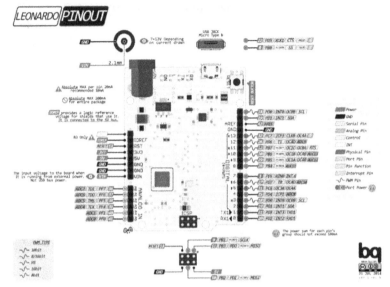

Figure 22 Pin out Arduino Leonardo

 In addition to many details, it is very important that the lines of the I²C bus are not connected to A5 and A4, but instead to IO2 and IO3 or own connections. The SPI bus is accessible only via the six-pin ICSP header. When using Arduino Shields take these changes into account.

To get the possibility to adapt older shields to the new Arduino Leonardo/Yún IO pin mapping, the Australian company Gorilla-Builderz developed and offers the LeoShield (https://www.gorilladistribution.com.au/product/leoshield/; Figure 23).

Older shields were developed for Arduino UNO, Duemilanove and other boards based on the ATmega168/328, and do not fit the ATmega32u4 used on Arduino Leornardo and Yún.

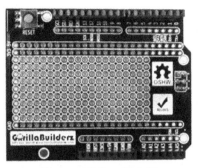

Figure 23 LeoShield

Using LeoShield, a large selection of older Arduino shields can be used on Arduino Leonardo and Yún. In general, this is possible without code changes or new libraries.

3.1.1 Hello World

For an initial startup of a new or newly installed development environment, one often uses Hello World programs.

For a microcontroller, a blinking LED and/or an output to a display can show us that the development environment is installed completely, the program upload to the target operates and the program is running in the microcontroller without any errors and is representing the functionality of such a Hello World function.

Listing 1 shows the source of the program *blink.ino*. The LED connected to IO13 will be on for 20 msec and off for two seconds, followed by the serial output of the character *.

```
/* Blink
Turns an LED on for a short time, then off for
two seconds, repeatedly. This example code is in
the public domain.
*/

// Pin 13 has an LED connected on most Arduino boards.
const int led = 13;

// the setup routine runs once when you press reset
void setup()
{
  // initialize the digital pin as an output.
  pinMode(led, OUTPUT);
```

```
  // initialize serial port
  Serial.begin(9600);
}

// the loop routine runs over and over again forever
void loop()
{
  digitalWrite(led, HIGH);   // turn the LED on
  delay(20);                 // wait for 20 ms
  digitalWrite(led, LOW);    // turn the LED off
  delay(2000);               // wait for 2 seconds
  Serial.write("*");
}
```

Listing 1 Source code *blink.ino*

3.1.2   Interrupt-driven Digital Input

For digital Input/Output, we have the functions `digital-Write()` and `digitalRead()`. If we want to use buttons for input, then we must consider that mechanical contacts bounce.

The Arduino tutorials describe debouncing by consecutively arranged queries and their comparison (http://arduino.cc/en/Tutorial/Debounce).

The interrupt-driven digital input is an alternative variant, which avoids additional time delay and affects the running program only when a key press triggers an interrupt. The interrupt service routine (ISR) handles this interrupt and changes the state in question.

We want to use both external interrupts INT0 (IO3) and INT1 (IO2) to query keys. If you want to query more keys, then this can be done with the help of interrupts PCINTx. In [4], the procedure in question is described.

For the handling of the interrupts INT0 and INT1, the Arduino knows the functions `attachInterrupt(interrupt, function, mode)` and `detachInterrupt(interrupt, function, mode)` hiding the complete register handling.

In the program sample *ExternalInterrupt.ino* (Listing 2), the serial data output as well as the state of the connected LED will be controlled by both interrupts.

```
// Title    : External Interrupt
// Author   : Claus Kuehnel
```

```
// Date     : 2014-02-09
// Id       : ExternalInterrupt.ino
// Version  : Arduino Yún 1.5.7
// based on :
//
// DISCLAIMER:
// The author is in no way responsible for any problems or
// damage caused by using this code. Use at your own risk.
//
// LICENSE:
// This code is distributed under the GNU Public License,
// which can be found at
// http://www.gnu.org/licenses/gpl.txt
//

const int pLED = 13;          // LED at Pin13
const int pINT0 = 3;          // INT0 at Pin3
const int pINT1 = 2;          // INT1 at Pin2

volatile boolean iflag;
int idx = 0;

void setup()
{
  Serial.begin(19200);
  pinMode(pLED, OUTPUT);

  pinMode(pINT0, INPUT);
  digitalWrite(pINT0, HIGH);   // Pull-up active

  pinMode(pINT1, INPUT);
  digitalWrite(pINT1, HIGH);   // Pull-up active

  delay(4000);

  // INT0 stops serial output
  attachInterrupt(0, stop_serial, FALLING);
  Serial.print("EICRA: ");
  Serial.println(EICRA, HEX);

  // INT1 resumes serial output
  attachInterrupt(1, resume_serial, FALLING);
  Serial.print("EICRA: ");
  Serial.println(EICRA, HEX);
  Serial.println("Setup finished.");
```

```
  resume_serial();
}

void loop()
{
  // iflag controls serial output
  if (iflag) Serial.println(idx);
  idx++;
  delay(1000);
}

void stop_serial()
{
  iflag = false;
  digitalWrite(pLED, HIGH);
}

void resume_serial()
{
  iflag = true;
  digitalWrite(pLED, LOW);
}
```

Listing 2 Source code *ExternalInterrupt.ino*

The interrupts INT0 and INT1 are fix-linked to the inputs IO3 and IO2 of the Arduino Yún. The pins in question are declared as constants.

The function setup() initializes both pins as input with pull-up resistors. The interrupt INT0 is linked to the function stop_serial() and INT1 to the function resume_serial(). The global interrupt is enabled by initialization already; therefore, no explicit enabling is needed here.

At the end of the setup, the register EICRA contains the value 0x0A. Both inputs will request an interrupt on a falling edge of the signal on these pins.

In the main loop loop() of this program sample, an index is incremented. The output of the index value can be stopped by INT0 and released by INT1. The connected LED signals the state in question.

Figure 24 shows the terminal output of this program sample. At start, you can see the initialization of the involved register. The output of the index value stops with a value of three after pressing the key connected to INT0. After pressing the key connected to INT1 the output continues. The index value now already has a value of nine.

If you want to trigger a state change using buttons, then the explained interrupt method is a very good approach.

Figure 24 Terminal output of the program *ExternalInterrupt.ino*

3.1.3 Query of Sensors

To get information from the environment, often sensors are queried, representing the sensed conditions in different ways.

In many cases, we get the detected signal as an analog voltage, which can be converted with the internal or an external AD converter in a format that can be processed by the Arduino Yún.

The temperature sensors of the LM135 series provide an output voltage proportional to the temperature of +10 mV/K. With less than 1Ω dynamic impedance, the device operates over a current range of 400 μA to 5 mA with virtually no change in performance. When calibrated at 25°C, the LM135 has typically less than 1°C error over a 100°C temperature range (http://www.ti.com/lit/ds/symlink/lm135.pdf).

The temperature sensors TMP35/TMP36/TMP37 have an output voltage proportional to the Celsius temperature scale. These sensors do not need an external calibration to get an accuracy of typically ±1°C at +25°C and ±2°C over a temperature range from −40°C to +125°C.

The supply current runs well below 50 μA (0.5 μA in shutdown), providing very low self-heating of less than 0.1°C in still air.

Table 2 shows the output characteristics of the three sensors. The output voltage of TMP35 is directly proportional to the temperature in 1/10°C without offset and, therefore, is almost ideal for our purposes here. The technical data of these sensors can be found on the website of Analog Devices at http://www.analog.com/media/en/technical-documentation/data-sheets/TMP35_36_37.pdf.

Sensor	Offset Voltage (V)	Output Voltage Scaling (mV/grd)	Output Voltage at 25°C (mV)
TMP35	0	10	250
TMP36	0.5	10	750
TMP37	0	20	500

Table 2 TMP3x output characteristics

The temperature sensors are available in different packaging. If you decide on the TO-92 package, you get very easy connectivity in the experimental environment. Table 3 shows how to connect LM335 and TMP35.

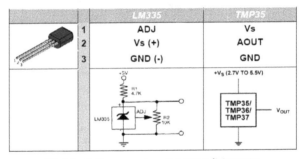

		LM335	TMP35
	1	ADJ	Vs
	2	Vs (+)	AOUT
	3	GND (-)	GND

Table 3 Connecting LM335/TMP35

If you use the LM335 without calibration, you get the following connection options on Arduino Yún (Table 4).

Analog pin A1 is connected to the signal output of one of the temperature sensors. To power the sensors with voltage, pin A0 is initialized as digital output and is switched on (HIGH). Pin A2 is initialized as digital output too, but is switched off (LOW) to feed GND to the sensors.

The resulting accuracy of the temperature measurement can be somewhat reduced because of the non-ideal properties of this type of connection.

	TMP35	IO	LM335	IO
A0	Vs	DOUT, HIGH		DOUT, HIGH *)
A1	AOUT	AIN	Vs	AIN *)
A2	GND	DOUT, LOW	GND	DOUT, LOW
A3				
A4				
A5				
				*) Vs via 4.7 kΩ to +5V

Table 4 Header direct connection

The program sample *LM335A_test.ino* (Listing 3) used a conventional connection of the sensors. The signal output Vs of the sensors was connected to the analog input AIN0 and +5 V respectively GND were connected directly with the Arduino Yún pins.

The program sample is quite simple. After the initialization of the serial interface, the following activities are embedded into the main loop:

- Query the AD converter (channel AIN0)
- Scaling of the measured value
- Correcting the offsets (CORR)
- Serial output of the temperature in K
- Conversion of the temperature into °C (OFS)
- Serial output of the temperature in °C
- Repeat all after a three-second waiting period

```
const int AIN = 0;
const int OFS = 273;
const int CORR = 29;

void setup()
{
  Serial.begin(9600);
  Serial.println("starting");
}
```

```
void loop()
{
  int value = analogRead(AIN);
  float temp = (value * 500.0/1024) - CORR;

  Serial.print("Kelvin: ");
  Serial.print(temp); // get temperature in Kel-
vin
  Serial.print("\tCelsius: ");
  Serial.println(temp - OFS); //get temp. in Celsius
  delay(3000);
}
```

Listing 3 Source code *LM335A_test.ino*

The device DHT22 is a sensor for temperature and humidity with digital output. A thermistor measures the temperature and a capacitive humidity sensor measures humidity (Figure 25 DHT22; http://meteobox.tk/files/AM2301.pdf).

Figure 25 DHT22

The measured result will be transferred serially via only one pin. The serial interface is highly sensitive to the timing and is incompatible with the Dallas 1-Wire protocol.

Using the Adafruit's DHT sensor library (https://github.com/adafruit/DHT-sensor-library), the access to these sensors becomes very easy, as the following program sample *DHTtester.ino* (Listing 4) shows.

Using the DHT22, the following characteristics are achievable:

- Maximum current consumption of 2.5 mA during conversion
- Accuracy of humidity measurement between 2 and 5 % for relative humidity 0 to 100 %
- Accuracy of temperature measurement of $\pm$ 0.5°C from -40 to 80°C
- Sample rate of 0.5 Hz (one measure in two seconds)
- Power supply of 3–5 V

The wiring of the pins of the DHT22 can be found in the source code of the sample program *DHTtester.ino* (Listing 4).

```
// Example testing sketch for various DHT
// humidity/temperature sensors
// Written by ladyada, public domain
// Modifications by Claus Kühnel 2014-01-25

#include <DHT.h>

// Pin 13 has an LED connected on most Arduino boards.
const int led = 13;

#define DHTPIN 2    // what pin we're connected to

// Uncomment whatever type you're using!
//#define DHTTYPE DHT11   // DHT 11
#define DHTTYPE DHT22   // DHT 22 (AM2302)
//#define DHTTYPE DHT21   // DHT 21 (AM2301)

// connect pin 1 (on the left) of the sensor to +5V
// connect pin 2 of the sensor to whatever your DHTPIN is
// connect pin 4 (on the right) of the sensor to GROUND
// connect a 10K resistor from pin 2 (data) to pin 1
// (power) of the sensor

DHT dht(DHTPIN, DHTTYPE);

void setup()
{
  // initialize the digital pin as an output.
  pinMode(led, OUTPUT);
```

```
  // initialize serial interface
  Serial.begin(9600); delay(4000);
  Serial.print("Test of DHT");
  Serial.print(DHTTYPE);
  Serial.println(" Sensor");

  dht.begin();
}

void loop()
{
  // turn the LED on (HIGH is the voltage level)
  digitalWrite(led, HIGH);
  // Reading temperature or humidity takes about 250 milli-
seconds!
  // Sensor readings may also be up to two seconds 'old'
(it's a very slow sensor)
  float h = dht.readHumidity();
  float t = dht.readTemperature();
  // turn the LED off by making the voltage LOW
  digitalWrite(led, LOW);
  // check if returns are valid,
  //if they are NaN (not a number), then some-
thing went wrong!
  if (isnan(t) || isnan(h))
  {
    Serial.println("Failed to read from DHT");
  }
  else
  {
    Serial.print("Humidity: ");
    Serial.print(h);
    Serial.print(" %\t");
    Serial.print("Temperature: ");
    Serial.print(t); Serial.println(" *C");
  }
  delay(1000);
}
```

Listing 4 Source code *DHTtester.ino*

The methods `dht.readHumidity()` and `dht.readTemperature()` encapsulate the access to the sensors. Both methods deliver the result of the query as a floating point number (float). Prior to both queries, an LED is switched on. After the queries, the LED is switched off. Thereafter, the output of humidity in percentage and the temperature in °C delivers the measured data to the serial interface (Figure **26**).

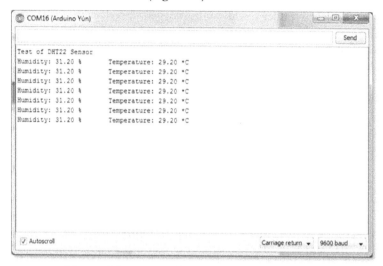

Figure 26 Output of program *DHTtester.ino*

3.1.4 Ardunio Weather Shield

The Weather Shield is an easy-to-use Arduino shield that grants access to barometric pressure, relative humidity, luminosity and temperature (https://www.sparkfun.com/products/12081). Figure 27 shows the Sparkfun Weather Shield with the sensors and two status LEDs arranged in the middle of the board.

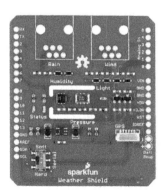

Figure 27 Sparkfun Weather Shield

Furthermore, on the shield, there are still contacts for the optional use of sensors for detecting wind speed and direction, rain and GPS for location and time available, but these cannot be directly connected to the Arduino Yún. If we can live without the external sensors, then the weather shield can be plugged directly with the Arduino Yún.

The weather shield has a supply voltage range of 3.3 to 16 V DC. The level adjustment to +5 V takes place on the board internally.

The weather shield contains the following sensors for which Arduino libraries are available:

Sensor	Physical property
HTU21D	Temperature/humidity
MPL3115A2	Barometric pressure
ALS-PT19	Luminosity (light)

The weather shield program samples use the libraries HTU21D and MPL3115A2, which can be downloaded from the URL https://dlnmh9ip6v2uc.cloudfront.net/assets/b/5/9/7/f/52cd8187c e395fa7158b456c.zip and installed into the Arduino library folder.

When the weather shield must be connected to the Arduino Yún, several things have to be considered:

The supply voltage for the I²C devices on the weather shield is derived from VIN. If the Arduino Yún is sourced via USB, then one has to connect VIN to 5 VDC externally. Since the Dragino Yún shield should be sourced via VIN, this connection is not required.

The I²C lines SDA and SCL are at the weather shield on pins A4 and A5. For Arduino Yún, SDA and SCL are on IO2 and IO3. An external connection of A4 and A5 with IO2 and IO3 is required.

The blue LED on the weather shield is connected to IO7. On this pin, Arduino Yún has a handshake signal and the pin should be not used. Therefore, the blue LED is not used here. Alternatively, the green LED can take over the function of the blue LED.

With these precautions, it is now possible to adapt one of the existing program examples. Listing 5 shows the source code of the program *weather_mini.ino*, which offers limited access to the board's internal sensors and outputs the results serially in a sequence defined by the constant PERIOD. The output of the sample program is shown in Figure 28.

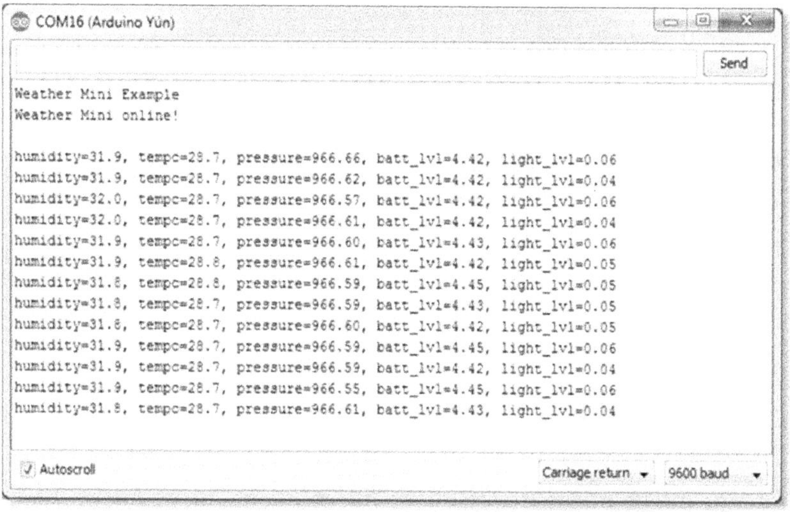

Figure 28 Output of program *weather_mini.ino*

```
/*
Weather Mini is a program example
- minimized to the internal sensors and
- adapted for use on Arduino Yún

By: Claus Kuehnel; 2014-10-04

Weather Shield Example
By: Nathan Seidle
SparkFun Electronics
Date: November 16, 2013
License: This code is public domain but you buy
me a beer if you use this and we meet someday
(Beerware license).

Much of this is based on Mike Grusin's USB
Weather Board code:
https://www.sparkfun.com/products/10586

This code reads the following sensors
(temperature in °C, humidity, pressure,
light_lvl, batt_lvl) and reports it over the
serial comm port.
This can be easily routed to a datalogger (such
as OpenLog) or a wireless transmitter (such as
```

```
 Electric Imp).
*/

#include <Wire.h>        //I2C needed for sensors
#include "MPL3115A2.h"   //Pressure sensor
#include "HTU21D.h"      //Humidity sensor

//Create an instance of the pressure sensor
MPL3115A2 myPressure;

//Create an instance of the humidity sensor
HTU21D myHumidity;

//Hardware pin definitions
//-----------------------------------------------
-
// digital I/O pins
// const byte STAT1 = 7; Do not use-Handshk on Arduino Yun
const byte STAT2 = 8;

// analog I/O pins
const byte REFERENCE_3V3 = A3;
const byte LIGHT = A1;
const byte BATT = A2;

//Global Variables
//-----------------------------------------------
-
//The millis counter to see when a second rolls
by
long lastSecond;
float humidity = 0; // %
float tempc = 0;     // temperature °C
float pressure = 0;
float light_lvl = 0;
float batt_lvl = 0; // analog value from 0 to
1023

//Defines
//-----------------------------------------------
-
#define PERIOD 2000

//-----------------------------------------------
-
```

```
void setup()
{
  Serial.begin(9600);
  delay(4000);
  Serial.println("Weather Mini Example");

// pinMode(STAT1, OUTPUT); //Status LED Blue
  pinMode(STAT2, OUTPUT); //Status LED Green

  pinMode(REFERENCE_3V3, INPUT);
  pinMode(LIGHT, INPUT);

  //configure the pressure sensor
  myPressure.begin(); // get sensor online
  //measure pressure in Pascals from 20 to 110
kPa
  myPressure.setModeBarometer();
  // set oversample to the recommended 128
  myPressure.setOversampleRate(7);
  // enable all three press and temp event flags
  myPressure.enableEventFlags();

  //configure the humidity sensor
  myHumidity.begin();

  lastSecond = millis();

  Serial.println("Weather Mini online!");
}

void loop()
{
  //keep track of PERIOD
  if(millis() - lastSecond >= PERIOD)
  {
    digitalWrite(STAT2, HIGH); //Blink stat LED

    //report all readings every second
    printWeather();

    digitalWrite(STAT2, LOW); //Turn off stat LED
    lastSecond = millis();
  }
  delay(200);
}
```

```
//calculates each of the variables that wunder-
ground is expecting
void calcWeather()
{
  //calc humidity
  humidity = myHumidity.readHumidity();

  //calc tempf from pressure sensor
  tempc = myPressure.readTemp();

  //calc pressure in hPa
  pressure = myPressure.readPressure()/100;

  //calc light level
  light_lvl = get_light_level();

  //calc battery level
  batt_lvl = get_battery_level();
}

//returns the voltage of the light sensor based
//on the 3.3V rail
//this allows us to ignore what VCC might be
//(an Arduino plugged into USB has VCC of 4.5 to 5.2V)
float get_light_level()
{
  float operatingVoltage =
analogRead(REFERENCE_3V3);

  float lightSensor = analogRead(LIGHT);

  //the reference voltage is 3.3V
  operatingVoltage = 3.3 / operatingVoltage;
  lightSensor = operatingVoltage * lightSensor;

  return(lightSensor);
}

//returns the volts of the raw pin based on the 3.3 V rail
//this allows us to ignore what VCC might be
//(an Arduino plugged into USB has VCC of 4.5 to 5.2V)
//battery level is connected to the RAW pin on Arduino
//and is fed through two 5% resistors:
//3.9K on the high side (R1), and 1K on the low side (R2)
```

```
float get_battery_level()
{
  float operatingVoltage =
analogRead(REFERENCE_3V3);

  float rawVoltage = analogRead(BATT);

  //the reference voltage is 3.3V
  operatingVoltage = 3.30 / operatingVoltage;

  rawVoltage = operatingVoltage * rawVoltage;
  //convert the 0 to 1023 int to actual voltage on BATT
pin

  rawVoltage *= 4.90; //(3.9k+1k)/1k - multiple
BATT voltage by the voltage divider to get actual
system voltage

  return(rawVoltage);
}


//prints the various variables directly to the port
//I don't like the way this function is written but Arduino
//does not support floats under sprintf
void printWeather()
{
  calcWeather(); //Go calc all the various sen-
sors

  Serial.println();
  Serial.print("humidity=");
  Serial.print(humidity, 1);
  Serial.print(", tempc=");
  Serial.print(tempc, 1);
  Serial.print(", pressure=");
  Serial.print(pressure, 2);
  Serial.print(", batt_lvl=");
  Serial.print(batt_lvl, 2);
  Serial.print(", light_lvl=");
  Serial.print(light_lvl, 2);
}
```

Listing 5 Source code of program *weather_mini.ino*

3.1.5 Internal ADC and PWM as DAC

The Arduino Yún has 12 analog inputs ADC0 to ADC5 and ADC8 to ADC13. If an Arduino Leonardo is used with the Dragino Yún shield, then the number of analog inputs remains unchanged. For all other Arduinos, this number is determined by the AVR controller used.

If fewer analog inputs are needed, then the unused analog inputs can also be used as GPIO (General Purpose I/O). Figure 21 showed the alternative functions for the IO pins of the Arduino Yún and Figure 22 the same for the Arduino Leonardo. The analog inputs are provided as well as all other pins with selectable pull-up resistors. But since an enabled pull-up resistor affects the AD conversion, it must be disabled during operation in case of analog input. Likewise, errors are to be expected if the connection had been previously configured as a digital output.

In the following program sample *adda.ino*, an output voltage is generated by PWM and filtered by an RC combination to a DC voltage. The AD converter captures this voltage and the conversion result should be equal to the value of the DA conversion.

Figure 29 shows the circuitry around the PWM output and the AD converter input for an Arduino 2009. The circuit for Arduino Yún is the same.

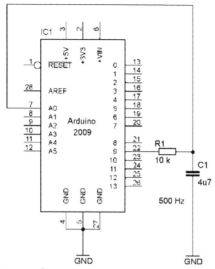

Figure 29 AD/DA conversion by internal resources

The PWM frequency for Arduino Yún is about 500 Hz. In practice, the RC combination (low pass) should be defined by the following formula:

$$\tau = R * C = \frac{(1 \dots 100)}{f_{PWM}}$$

If you choose the time constant τ as too high, then the settling time increases. If you choose it too low, however, then the filter effect is too low.

The selected time constant of 47 ms according to Figure 29 is at the lower end; hence, an optimal filtering effect can be expected. But to demonstrate the principle of AD conversion should suffice here.

In the program sample *adda.ino* (Listing 6), the instruction `analogWrite(AOUT,i)` generates a PWM on I/O9, the analog input AIN0 captures the filtered value for AD conversion and, after a delay of one second (`delay(1000)`), the function `analogRead(AIN0)` reads the result of the AD conversion in an endless loop. The remaining instructions are only for serial output or configuration.

One point must be considered. For the PWM, the eight-bit timer Timer1 is used, so that only values between 0 and 255 can be set here. The internal AD converter has a resolution of 10 bits and its results are between 0 and 1023. We have to consider a factor of four for the calculation of the deviation (ADC-4DAC).

```
const int AOUT = 9;   // IO9 is PWM output
const int AIN0 = 0;   // AIN0 is analog input

void setup()
{
  pinMode(AOUT, OUTPUT); //configure PWM as out-
put
  Serial.begin(19200);
  Serial.println("DAC\tADC\tADC-4DAC");
}

void loop()
{
  int i, val;
  for (i=0; i<256; i+=8)
  {
    analogWrite(AOUT, i);      // set PWM to  0-255
    delay(1000);
    Serial.print(i);          // output DAC value
    Serial.print("\t");
    // read result of ADC channel AIN0
    val = analogRead(AIN0);
    Serial.print(val);        // output ADC value
    Serial.print("\t");
    Serial.println(val - 4*i);// calc difference
  }
}
```

Listing 6 Source code *adda.ino*

After the start of the program *adda.ino*, we can see the output of the results in the monitor. Figure 30 shows the serial output of the individual runs through the loop. The third column lists the calculated deviation ADC–4*DAC, which has a principal character only due to the less ideal RC filtering.

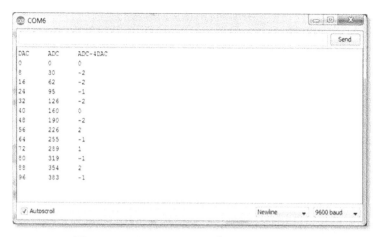

Figure 30 Output of DA/AD conversion

3.1.6 Internal ADC in Free Running Mode

The internal AD converter of the Arduino can not only operate in single conversion mode but also in free running mode. For the initialization of the free running mode and the reading out of the result of the AD conversion, we must access the registers in question directly. Other examples of the access to such registers, as it is also required for the use of interrupts, can be found in [4].

Several registers are responsible for the operation of the AD converter. At this point, only the initialization used here can be considered. To examine all options, the comprehensive data sheet of ATmega32u4 must be used [5].

	7	6	5	4	3	2	1	0
ADCSRA	ADEN	ADSC	ADATE	ADIF	ADIE	ADPS2	ADPS1	ADPS0

In register ADCSRA, the AD converter will be enabled (ADEN), the first AD conversion will be started (ADSC) and the auto trigger required for the free running mode will be enabled (ADATE).The bits ADPS2–ADPS0 define the pre-scaler for the clock of the AD converter.

To ensure a maximum resolution of the AD conversion, the internal circuitry should operate with an AD conversion clock between 50 and 200 kHz. If all pre-scaler bits are set, then the 16 MHz system clock is divided by 128 and an AD conversion clock of 125 kHz results.

From timing diagram (Figure 31), one can see that the AD conversion ends after 13 clock cycles; with the used pre-scaler, the conversion time is about 100μs.

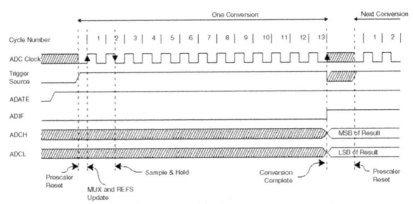

Figure 31 Timing diagram of free running mode

	7	6	5	4	3	2	1	0
ADMUX	REFS1	REFS0	ADLAR	MUX4	MUX3	MUX2	MUX1	MUX0

The register ADMUX can select the used analog channel (MUX4–MUX0) and the analog reference voltage (REFS1, REFS0) additionally.

We work here using AVcc = 2.56 V as the reference voltage. The data format can be left or right aligned. In the register, ADCSRB is still the bit MUX5, which must be considered in some cases, as in function setADC(), for example (Table 5).

MUX5-0	Single-ended Input
000000	ADC0
000001	ADC1
000100	ADC4
000101	ADC5
000110	ADC6
000111	ADC7
011110	1.1 V (Band gap)
011111	0 V(GND)
100000	ADC8
100001	ADC9
100010	ADC10
100011	ADC11
100100	ADC12
100101	ADC13
100111	Temperature Sensor

Table 5 Multiplexer Initialization for single-ended input

As Table 5 shows, the analog inputs are not limited to the accessible input pins ADCx. For the first tests, the internal bandgap reference, the internal ground and the temperature sensor are important options. These sources will be queried as known input voltages in the next program sample.

The setup of both registers of the AD converter can be seen most easily from the source code of the program sample *free_running_adc.ino* (Listing 7).

```
// Title    : InternalADC in Free Running Mode
// Author   : Claus Kühnel
// Date     : 2013-09-18
// Id       : free_running_adc.ino
// Version  : 1.5.7
// Micro    : Arduino Yún
//
// DISCLAIMER:
// The author is in no way responsible for any problems or
```

```
// damage caused by
// using this code. Use at your own risk.
//
// LICENSE:
// This code is distributed under the GNU Public License,
// which can be found at
// http://www.gnu.org/licenses/gpl.txt
// ------------------------------------------------
-


// ADMUX with internal 2.56 V VREF
#define ADC0 0xC0
#define ADC1 0xC1
#define ADC4 0xC4
#define ADC5 0xC5

#define BANDGAP 0xDE
#define GND 0xDF
#define TEMP 0xC7

const int T1 = 25;  // °C
const int C1 = 313; // ADC count @ 25°C

// ADCSRA
#define FREE_RUNNING_MODE ((1<<ADEN) | (1<<ADSC) |
(1<<ADATE) | (1<<ADPS2) | (1<<ADPS1) | (1<<ADPS0))

#define PURPOSE "Test of Free Running ADC"

const byte LED = 13;

word adc_value;

void setADC(byte config)
{
  ADCSRA &= ~(1<<ADEN); ADMUX = config;
  ADCSRA = FREE_RUNNING_MODE;
  if (config==TEMP) ADCSRB |= (1<<MUX5);
  else
    ADCSRB &= ~(1<<MUX5);
}

word getADC(void)
{
  return (ADCL | (ADCH << 8));
```

```
}

void printResult(void)
{
  digitalWrite(LED, 1);           // LED on
  delay(100);
  adc_value = getADC();
  digitalWrite(LED, 0);           // LED off
  Serial.print(adc_value, HEX); //output ADC value
  Serial.print("\t");
  // calc voltage and output
  Serial.print((float) adc_value*2.56/1023);
  Serial.println(" V");
}

void setup()
{
  delay(2000);
  pinMode(LED, OUTPUT);
  Serial.begin(9600);
  delay(4000);
  Serial.println(PURPOSE);
}

void loop()
{
  Serial.print("Bandgap-Referenz ");
  setADC(BANDGAP);
  printResult();
  Serial.print("GND           ");
  setADC(GND); printResult();
  Serial.print("Temperature    ");
  setADC(TEMP);
  printResult();
  Serial.print("   Temperature approx. ");
  Serial.print(adc_value-C1+T1);
  Serial.print(" grd C\n");
  delay(2000);
}
```

Listing 7 Source code *free_running_adc.ino*

In several definitions, the different initializations of the registers of the AD converter are noted. The function setADC() handles the configuration of the analog multiplexer according to Table 5.

Before changing the register configuring the multiplexer, the AD converter will be disabled. After the configuration, the AD converter will be enabled again and the first AD conversion will be started. Following this start, the AD converter is in the free running mode. This means that, at the end of an AD conversion, the result will be written into the registers ADCH and ADCL and the next conversion will begin. The function getADC() reads these registers in the order ADCL followed by ADCH.

In the main loop loop(), the inputs Bandgap Reference, Ground (GND) and temperature sensor are queried and the result is sent to the serial output.

To get reliable measurement values from the internal temperature sensor, it must be calibrated. A very simple offset adjustment was made here. To increase the accuracy of the temperature measurement, a more complex calibration is required. These calibration procedures are described, for example, in [6] and [7].

The function printResult() outputs the results of the AD conversions. Figure 32 shows the output of this program sample.

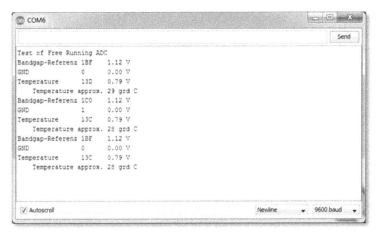

Figure 32 Output of program *free_running_adc.ino*

3.1.7   AD/DA Module PCF8591

Arduino Yún has an internal 12-channel 10-bit AD converter, which must share its input pins with the digital input/output pins (IO). An external AD/DA sub-system can offer flexibility for simple tasks.

The integrated circuit PCF8591 is a simple 8-bit AD/DA module with four analog inputs and one analog output controlled by the I²C bus. The complete data sheet can be downloaded from the website of the manufacturer NXP (http://www.nxp.com/documents/data_sheet/PCF8591.pdf).

Figure 33 shows a compact module with a potentiometer for analog input, temperature and light sensor, and an LED connected to the analog output. Amazon.com et al. offer this module.

Jumpers connect the sensors and the LED to the PCF8591. When disconnecting them, the pins are free for GPIO.

Figure 33 PCF8591 module

The module has three address lines, whereby up to eight of these modules can be connected to the same I²C bus.

In accordance to the I²C specifications, the PCF8591 uses a 7-bit slave address. The higher four bits are internally determined, while the lower three bits are determined by the logic levels on the address pins A2–A0. Therefore, we get an address range from 72 (0x48) to 79 (0x4F) dependent on the logic pattern of the bits A2–A0.

1	0	0	1	A2	A1	A0
MSB						LSB

By default, the address pins of the module are on GND, which defines a device address of 72 used in the program sample *PCF8591_Moduletest.ino* (Listing 8).

The Wire library encapsulates the access to the I²C bus and must be included at the beginning of the program by the instruction

`#include<Wire.h>`. The function `setup()` initializes the functionality of the libraries Wire and Serial.

In the function `loop()`, the instruction `readWire(72, channel)` queries the potentiometer, the temperature sensor and photo resistor followed by the output of the resulting values.

As a last action, the instruction `writeWire(72,Aout)` outputs the analog value `Aout` increased by 10 in each loop while below 250. After a waiting time of 100 ms, the next run through the loop begins.

The functions `readWire()` and `writeWire()` transpose the I²C bus protocol according to the data sheet. The function `readWire()` requests six bytes from PCF8591. The right result is with the second byte that is available already.

The staircase-wise changing output voltage can be monitored on line OUT by a multimeter or by the changing illumination of the connected LED when the jumper is connected.

```
#include <Wire.h>

void setup()
{
  Wire.begin();
  Serial.begin(9600);
}

int Aout = 0;

void loop()
{
  int pot = readWire(72,0x41);
  int temp = readWire(72,0x42);
  int light = readWire(72,0x43);

  Serial.print(pot,DEC);
  Serial.print("\t");
  Serial.print(temp,DEC);
  Serial.print("\t");
  Serial.println(light,DEC);

  if (Aout < 250)    Aout += 10;
  else               Aout = 0;

  writeWire(72,0x40,Aout);
```

```
  delay(100);
}

int readWire(int device, int channel)
{
  int retval;
  Wire.beginTransmission(device);
  Wire.write(channel);
  Wire.endTransmission();

  Wire.requestFrom(device, 6);

  while (Wire.available())
  {
    retval = Wire.read();
  }
  return retval;
}

void writeWire(int device, int channel, int value)
{
  Wire.beginTransmission(device);
  Wire.write(channel);
  Wire.write(value);
  Wire.endTransmission();
}
```

Listing 8 Source code *PCF8591_Moduletest.ino*

3.1.8   LCD

Inexpensive text LCDs can be used to implement simple display functions. Such displays are available with different interfaces to the controlling microcontroller.

For the display functions here, I used a LCD2041 text LCD (four lines with 20 characters) with an I²C bus interface. Figure 34 shows the different display options of this well-appointed text LCD.

Figure 34 Display options LCD2041 (MatrixOrbital)

For the purpose of controlling the LCD2041 by an Arduino, the Library *MatrixOrbitali2c* exists. The library can be downloaded from the GitHub repository and installed in the Library directory (https://github.com/bkonosky/Arduino-Matrix-Orbital-i2c-library).

I cannot discuss the commands here in detail but the program sample *LCD2041_Test.ino* (Listing 9) shows their use. More details can be found in the Library files.

The function setup() initializes the baud rate of the serial interface (9600 baud) and the number of lines and columns as well as the contrast of the LCD. The contrast can have a value between zero and 255. High values mean high contrast. The default after power-on is a contrast value of 128.

In the function loop(), successively the four functions TextOutput(), BigDigits(), WideVBargraph() and HBargraph() will be called after clearing the display. The function TextOutput() positions the cursor and outputs text. The function BigDigits() outputs big digits, which may be an option for readability from a distance. The function WideVBargraph() generates a vertical bar graph. On the abscissa, there is a maximum of 20 positions (20 columns) with a maximum of 32 units. The display values are scaled accordingly. At a suitable point, text can be inserted into the display as well. The function HBargraph() generates in a maximum of four columns a comprehensive horizontal bar graph. Here, the horizontal resolution is 100 units.

```
// Title    : Controlling LCD2041 via I2C
// Author   : Claus Kühnel
// Date     : 2013-10-08
// Id       : LCD2041_Test.ino
// Version  : 1.5.7
//
// DISCLAIMER:
// The author is in no way responsible for any problems or
// damage caused by
// using this code. Use at your own risk.
//
// LICENSE:
// This code is distributed under the GNU Public License,
// which can be found at
// http://www.gnu.org/licenses/gpl.txt

#include <Wire.h>
#include <MatrixOrbitali2c.h>

const int LED = 13;          // LED at Pin13

MatrixOrbitali2c lcd(0x5C >> 1);

void TextOutput()
{
  lcd.home();
  lcd.print("Arduino Yun");
  lcd.setCursor(1,2);
  lcd.print("writes text");
  lcd.setCursor(1,3);
  lcd.print("by I2C to LCD2041.");
  lcd.setCursor(1,4);
  lcd.print("www.arduino.cc");
}

void BigDigits()
{
  byte pos = 2;
  lcd.clear();
  lcd.initLargeDigits();
  for (int i=0; i<6; i++)
  {
    lcd.placeLargeDigit(pos,char(i));
    pos=pos + 3;
    delay(200);
```

```
  }
}

void WideVBargraph()
{
  lcd.clear();
  lcd.initWideVertical();
  for (int i=1; i<21; i++)
  {
    int j = i * 32; j = j / 20;
    lcd.drawVertical(i, j);
    delay(10);
  }
  lcd.setCursor(1,1);
  lcd.print("Bargraph");
}

void HBargraph()
{
  lcd.clear();
  lcd.initHorizontal();
  lcd.drawHorizontal(1,1,0,100);
  lcd.drawHorizontal(1,2,0,55);
  lcd.drawHorizontal(1,3,0,27);
  lcd.drawHorizontal(1,4,0,13);
  lcd.setCursor(12,4);
  lcd.print("Bargraph");
}

void setup()
{
  Serial.begin(9600);
  delay(4000);
  Serial.println("LCD2041 SETUP");
  lcd.begin(4,20);        // 4 lines 20 characters
  lcd.setContrast(180); // 0 - 255
}

void loop()
{
  lcd.clear();
  TextOutput();
  delay(2000);
  BigDigits();
  delay(2000);
```

```
  WideVBargraph();
  delay(2000);
  HBargraph();
  delay(2000);
}
```

Listing 9 Source code *LCD2041_Test.ino*

Another possibility for such an LCD is its use as a debugging display. The program sample *Debug_LCD.ino* (Listing 10) demonstrates this possibility.

```
// Title    : Debugging LCD with I2C interface
// Author   : Claus Kühnel
// Date     : 2013-10-08
// Id       : Debug_LCD.ino
// Version  : 1.5.7
//
// DISCLAIMER:
// The author is in no way responsible for any problems or
// damage caused by
// using this code. Use at your own risk.
//
// LICENSE:
// This code is distributed under the GNU Public License,
// which can be found at
// http://www.gnu.org/licenses/gpl.txt

#include <Wire.h>
#include <MatrixOrbitalI2c.h>

#define DEBUG 1

const int LED = 13;      // LED at Pin13 unsigned
int count = 65536;

MatrixOrbitalI2c lcd(0x5C >> 1);

void flash()
{
  static boolean output = HIGH;

  digitalWrite(LED, output);
  output = !output;
```

```
}

void setup()
{
  Serial.begin(9600);
  delay(4000);
  Serial.println("Application running...");
  lcd.begin(4,20);       // 4 lines 20 characters
  lcd.setContrast(180);  // 0-255
  lcd.clear();
  lcd.autoScroll();
  lcd.lineWrap();

  if (DEBUG) lcd.print("DEBUG LCD\n");
  else lcd.print("No Debug Info");
}

void loop()
{
  flash();
  delay(200);
  if (DEBUG)
  {
    lcd.print("Count = ");
    lcd.print(count);
    lcd.print("\n");
    count++;
  }
}
```

Listing 10 Source code *Debug_LCD.ino*

The directive #define DEBUG 1 controls the debugging output. If DEBUG is set to zero, then the debugging output is suppressed.

The function flash() toggles the LED connected to IO13. Toggling means switching off an illuminated LED or switching on a dark LED. Here in this program sample, the function flash() can be substituted by any other function called in the main loop periodically.

The function setup() initializes the baud rate of the serial interface and the LCD again. Due to the later use of the AutoScroll and LineWrap functionality, the initialization of the LCD is a little more extensive here.

If theAutoScroll function is activated and the display filled with characters, then the next character will be output in home position (top left position). An activated LineWrap function causes the character output in the next line, if the previous one is filled with characters. The function setup() informs by a message to the LCD whether debugging is activated or not.

In the main loop, the function flash() is called followed by a short delay time (delay(200)). The LED toggles in each cycle and blinks with 200 ms of on/off time.

In the debugging mode, a counter variable will be displayed on LCD and is incremented afterwards. This counter variable is almost pointless but is representative of a debugging output in the main loop.

3.2 Bridge Library

As described in Chapter 2.6, the Arduino Yún includes two processors, an ATmega32u4 and an Atheros AR9331. The Bridge library ensures that both processors can communicate and hides the implementation details from the user.

The Bridge library simplifies communication between the two processors (http://arduino.cc/en/Reference/YunBridgeLibrary). It is derived from the Stream library and many of the methods are already known from the Serial library.

Bridge commands from ATmega32u4 will be interpreted by Python on AtherosAR9331. Initiated by ATmega32u4, commands on the Linux side can be executed. Data exchange between both CPUs is organized by the shared memory.

Via the Bridge library, the ATmega32u4 is extended with functions that provide network connection and other functions of a Linux device. Conversely, the Linux device gains simpler and faster access to sensors and actuators through this microcontroller supplement.

The Bridge library contains several classes described in Table 6 (http://arduino.cc/en/Reference/YunBridgeLibrary). The usage of the different classes will be explained by some program samples.

Class	Description
Process	Process is used to launch processes on the Linux processor, and other things like shell scripts.
Console	Console can be used to communicate with the net-

	work monitor in the Arduino IDE, through a shell. Functionally, it is very similar to Serial.
FileIO	An interface to the Linux file system. Can be used to read/write files on the SD card
HttpClient	Creates an HTTP client on Linux. Acts as a wrapper for common CURL commands by extending Process.
Mailbox	An asynchronous, session-less interface for communicating between Linux and Arduino.
YunClient	An Arduino-based HTTP client, modeled after the EthernetClient class.
YunServer	An Arduino based HTTP server, modeled after the EthernetServer class.
Temboo	An interface to Temboo.com making it easy to connect to a large variety of online tools.
Spacebrew	Spacebrew is "a simple way to connect interactive things to one another" that uses WebSockets to communicate.

Table 6 Components of the Bridge library

3.2.1   Executing Linux Commands

The Process library can be used to start processes from ATmega32u4 on AtherosAR9331.

The program sample *runShellCommand.ino* (Listing 11) lists the content of the home directory of the Linux device AR9331 by executing the Linux command `ls /$HOME`.

The command `ls /$HOME`, which should be executed is declared as string variable `cmd` and initialized.

The function `runShellCommand()` prepares the call of the command and the handling of the expected return value. At first, the process `p`, which is responsible for the handling of the Linux device is initiated. The method `runShellCmd(cmd)` calls the shell script `ls /$HOME` on the Atheros AR9331 and as long as that process delivers data (`p.available()>0`), they will be read from the ATmega32u4 (`p.read`) and output character-wise via the serial interface (`Serial.print(c)`).

The function `runShellCmd()` is included into the function `setup()` and will be executed once after the start of the program. Before that, the Bridge library (`Bridge.begin()`) and the serial interface will be initialized. The function `loop()` has nothing to do after that.

Figure 35 shows the output of the program sample *runShellCommands.ino*.

```
// Title    : Running Shell Command
// Author   : Claus Kuehnel
// Date     : 2013-10-18
// Id       : runShellCommand.ino
// CPU      : Arduino Yun
// Version  : 1.5.7
//
// DISCLAIMER:
// The author is in no way responsible for any problems or
// damage caused by
// using this code. Use at your own risk.
//
// LICENSE:
// This code is distributed under the GNU Public License,
// which can be found at
// http://www.gnu.org/licenses/gpl.txt

#include <Process.h>

String cmd = "ls /$HOME";       // Shell Command

unsigned int runShellCmd(const String &cmd)
{
  Process p;

  p.runShellCommand(cmd);
  while (p.available()>0)
  {
    char c = p.read();
    Serial.print(c);
  }
  Serial.flush();
}

void setup()
{
```

```
  Bridge.begin();       // initialize the Bridge
  Serial.begin(9600);// initialize the Serial
Port

  // wait until a Serial Monitor is connected.
  while(!Serial);
  Serial.println("List Home directory on Linux
Device...");

  runShellCmd(cmd);
}

void loop()
{
  // nothing to do
}
```

Listing 11 Source code *runShellCommand.ino*

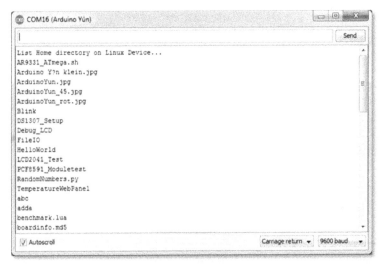

Figure 35 List Home Directory

If you want to access the Linux device via Ethernet or WiFi directly, then knowledge of the network addresses is required. If the IP address was received from the router via DHCP, then they may well have different values.

The Linux command ifconfig delivers this address and some more information. The program sample *ifconfig.ino* (Listing 12) queries these data by calling `ifconfig` and outputs them according to Figure 36.

Interesting for us here are only the network addresses for the Ethernet interface eth1 (192.168.1.30) and for WLAN wlan0 (192.168.1.3). Via these addresses, we can access the Linux device from the development PC via SSH. In Chapter 4.1.1, I will return to this.

```
// Title    : Running Shell Commands
// Author   : Claus Kuehnel
// Date     : 2013-10-18
// Id       : ifconfig.ino
// CPU      : Arduino Yun
// Version  : 1.5.7
//
// DISCLAIMER:
// The author is in no way responsible for any problems or
//damage caused by
// using this code. Use at your own risk.
//
// LICENSE:
// This code is distributed under the GNU Public License,
// which can be found at
// http://www.gnu.org/licenses/gpl.txt

#include <Process.h>

String cmd = "ifconfig"; // Shell Command

unsigned int runShellCmd(const String &cmd)
{
  Process p;
  p.runShellCommand(cmd);
  while (p.available()>0)
  {
    char c = p.read();
    Serial.print(c);
  }
  Serial.flush();
}

void setup()
{
  Bridge.begin();          // initialize the Bridge
```

```
  Serial.begin(9600);    // initialize the Serial

  // wait until a Serial Monitor is connected.
  while(!Serial);
  Serial.println("List available Network Inter-
faces...");

  runShellCmd(cmd);
}

void loop()
{
  // nothing to do
}
```

Listing 12 Source code *ifconfig.ino*

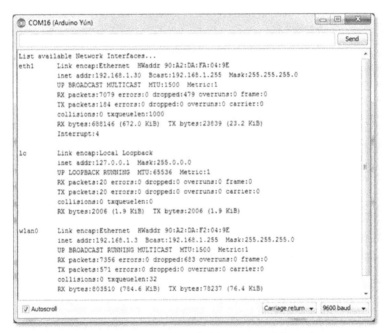

Figure 36 Output of available network interfaces

The program sample *cpuinfo.ino* (Listing 13) contains the function
runCpuInfo(). This calls the command cat
/proc/cpuinfo and the function runUptime(), which que-

ries the run time of the CPU after the last boot. The file
/proc/cpuinfo returns information to the CPU running on the
Linux device.

Since both functions are called once each, they were placed inside
the function setup(). The function loop() is empty for this
reason.

The pattern for calling the methods of the class Process is always
the same. Starting with p.begin("command"), the Linux command in question is defined. With p.addParameter ("parameter"), the command can be supplemented through additional
parameters. After completing the command, the processing of that
command in the Linux environment can be started by p.run().
The response of the called command can be read as long as the condition p.available()>0 is true.

```
/*
  Running process using Process class.

  This sketch demonstrates how to run Linux
  processes using an Arduino Yún.

  created 5 Jun 2013
  by Cristian Maglie

  Modifications
  by Claus Kühnel 2014-09-28

  This example code is in the public domain.
*/

#include <Process.h>

void setup()
{
  // initialize Bridge
  Bridge.begin();

  // initialize Serial
  Serial.begin(9600);

  // wait until a Serial Monitor is connected.
  while (!Serial);
```

```
  // run example processes
  runCpuInfo();
  runUptime();
}

void loop()
{
  // do nothing here.
}

void runCpuInfo()
{
  // launch "cat /proc/cpuinfo" command
  //(shows info on Atheros CPU)
  // cat is a command line utility that shows the content
  // of a file
  Process p;    // create a process and call it
"p"
  // process that launches the "cat" command
  p.begin("cat");
  // add the cpuinfo file path as parameter to
cat
  p.addParameter("/proc/cpuinfo");
  // run the process and wait for its termination
  p.run();

  Serial.println("CPU Info:");

  // print command output on the Serial
  // a process output can be read with the stream
  // methods
  while (p.available()>0)
  {
    char c = p.read();
    Serial.print(c);
  }
  // ensure the last bit of data is sent.
  Serial.flush();
}

void runUptime()
{
  Process p;    // create a process and call it
"p"
  p.runShellCommand("uptime");
```

```
// run the process and wait for its termination
p.run();
Serial.println("Uptime:");

// print command output on the Serial
// a process output can be read with the stream
// methods
while (p.available()>0)
{
  char c = p.read();
  Serial.print(c);
}
// ensure the last bit of data is sent.
Serial.flush();
}
```

Listing 13 Source code *cpuinfo.ino*

Figure 37 shows the output of data saved in file *cpuinfo*, which was queried by the Linux command cat/proc/cpuinfo and the response of the command uptime.

Chapter 4.2.1.1 will present detailed explanations for these outputs.

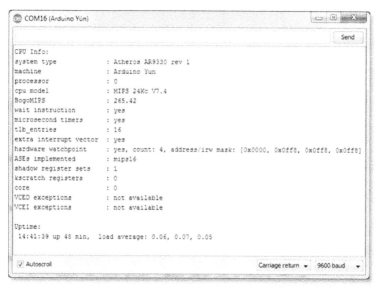

Figure 37 Output of program *cpuinfo.ino*

3.2.2 Execution of Scripts

The execution of scripts does not differ from the execution of Linux commands described in the last chapter.

However, these scripts must be made available once on the Linux device. The script itself can be Shell, Python or Lua scripts. How to handle such scripts is described in Section 4.2.

In the program sample *sendMail.ino*, the shell script *sendmail.sh* running on the AtherosAR9331 on Linino (OpenWRT) is called. Chapter 4.1.7 explains the shell script *sendmail.sh*, which sends emails via *cURL* from GoogleMail. For *cURL* also, I must refer here to Chapter 4.1.7.

Listing 14 shows the call of the shell script *sendmail.sh* from command p.runShellCommand(command). The desired command is notified completely here. The loop while(p.running()), waits for the end of the execution of the running command before the response of the command is evaluated.

```
//
// Title    : Send Mail via cURL
// Author   : Claus Kuehnel
// Date     : 2014-09-29
// Id       : sendMail.ino
// CPU      : Arduino Yun
// Version  : 1.5.7
//
// DISCLAIMER:
// The author is in no way responsible for any problems or
// damage caused by using this code. Use at your own risk.
//
// LICENSE:
// This code is distributed under the GNU Public License,
// which can be found at
// http://www.gnu.org/licenses/gpl.txt

#include <Process.h>

void setup()
{
  Bridge.begin();      // initialize the Bridge
  Serial.begin(9600);  // initialize the Serial

  // wait until a Serial Monitor is connected.
```

```
  while(!Serial);
  Serial.println("Sending Mail...");

  Process p;   // create a process and call it
"p"
  // call the script sendmail.sh
  p.runShellCommand("/$HOME/sendmail.sh");
  while(p.running());

  while (p.available()>0)
  {
    char c = p.read();
    Serial.print(c);
  }
  Serial.flush();
  Serial.println("End.");
}

void loop()
{
  // nothing to do
}
```

Listing 14 Source code *sendMail.ino*

Figure 38 shows the output of the program *sendMail.ino*. The first and last output lines are sent by the ATmega32u4 from Listing 14, while the second and third are sent by the shell script. Figure 39 shows the received mail.

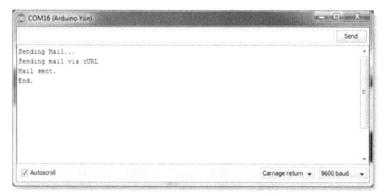

Figure 38 Output of program *sendMail.ino*

Figure 39 Received mail

The program sample *runShellCommands.ino* (Listing 15) shows how Lua and Python scripts on the AtherosAR9331 under Linino (OpenWRT) can be executed

Here, the script *date.lua* generates a formatted output of date and time and the script *RandomNumbers.py* generates 100 pseudo random numbers between zero and 100, and saves these in the file *random-numbers.txt*. The scripts will be considered in Chapters 4.2.3.1 and 4.2.2.1. Figure 40 shows the output of the program sample *runShell-Commands.ino.*

```
// Title    : Running Shell Commands
// Author   : Claus Kuehnel
// Date     : 2014-09-29
// Id       : runShellCommands.ino
// CPU      : Arduino Yun
// Version  : 1.5.7
//
// DISCLAIMER:
// The author is in no way responsible for any problems or
// damage caused by using this code. Use at your own risk.
//
// LICENSE:
// This code is distributed under the GNU Public License,
// which can be found at
// http://www.gnu.org/licenses/gpl.txt
```

```
#include <Process.h>

unsigned int runShellCmd(const String &cmd)
{
  Process p;

  p.runShellCommand(cmd);
  while(p.running());
  while (p.available() > 0)
  {
    char c = p.read(); Serial.print(c);
  }
  Serial.flush();
}

void setup()
{
  Bridge.begin();        // Initialize the Bridge
  Serial.begin(9600);    // Initialize the Serial

  // Wait until a Serial Monitor is connected.
  while(!Serial);
  Serial.println("Running Shell Commands...");

  runShellCmd("lua /$HOME/date.lua");
  Serial.println();
  runShellCmd("python /$HOME/RandomNumbers.py");
  Serial.println();
  runShellCmd("cat /$HOME/randomnumbers.txt");

  Serial.println("\nEnd.");
}

void loop()
{
  // nothing to do
}
```

Listing 15 Source code *runShellCommands.ino*

Figure 40 Output of program *runShellCommands.ino*

3.2.3 Writing and Reading Files

The Atheros AR9331 has much more memory than the ATmega32u4 and may be expanded beyond by a SD card or a memory stick. Therefore, it is of interest to use this memory from the Arduino side as well.

FileIO is the base class for writing and reading the memory of the Arduino Yún (Atheros AR9331). In the highest level of the SD card (root), an empty directory /arduino can be created and the Arduino Yún establishes a link to /mnt/sd.

Two simple program samples demonstrate the writing and reading of a text file. With the understanding of the mechanism, the subsequent program samples can be understood more easily.

Listing 16 (*write_file.ino*) shows the writing of data in a text file. Since one write process should follow, all actions are placed inside the function setup(). The function loop() is empty again.

At the beginning of the program sample *write_file.ino*, we load the FileIO library by #include<FileIO.h>. Thereafter, the initialization of the libraries Bridge and Serial, and the first output to the console follow.

Now, the more interesting part begins with the initialization of the file system by FileSystem.begin().

The write process begins by opening the file with path and file name and the kind of access as arguments (Filetxt=FileSystem.open("/tmp/test.txt",FILE

_WRITE);). The writing itself is called by txt.print() and txt.close() closes the file finally.

```
#include <FileIO.h>

void setup()
{
  Bridge.begin();
  Serial.begin(9600);

  // wait for Serial port to connect.
  while(!Serial);
  Serial.println("Write text file...");

  FileSystem.begin();
  File txt = FileSystem.open("/tmp/test.txt",
FILE_WRITE);
  txt.print("Das ist Text in einem Textfile");
  txt.close();    // close the file
  Serial.println("Text file written.");
}

void loop()
{
  // nothing to do here
}
```

Listing 16 Source code *write_file.ino*

Listing 17 (*read_file.ino*) shows the reading of data from a text file. The procedure is quite similar but, while opening the file, the kind of access is FILE_READ here.

If the file opening was not successful because the file possibly does not exist, then we get an error message "File open error" via the console and the program goes into an endless loop.

Otherwise, the content of the file will be read character by character (c=txt.read()), output to the console and concatenated to a string (str += c;).

If the file was read, then the output to the console and the closing of the file follow.

```
#include <FileIO.h>

void setup()
{
  Bridge.begin();
  Serial.begin(9600);

  // wait for Serial port to connect.
  while(!Serial);
  Serial.println("Read text file...");

  FileSystem.begin();
  File txt = FileSystem.open("/tmp/test.txt",
FILE_READ);
  if (!txt) Serial.print("File open error");
  else
  {
    String str = "";
    while(txt.available())
    {
        char c = txt.read();
        Serial.print(c);
        str += c;
    }
    txt.close();
    Serial.println("\nText file read.");
  }
}

void loop()
{
  // nothing to do here
}
```

Listing 17 Source code *read_file.ino*

The more complex program sample *FileIO.ino* (Listing 18) shows a function uploadScript(), which generates a script file. This script will be executed in function loop() by calling runScript().

The function uploadScript() generates a shell script *wlan-stats.sh* in directory /tmp.

The instructions `script.print("#!/bin/sh\n");` and `script.print("ifconfig wlan0 | grep 'RXbytes'\n");` build the following shell script:

```
#!/bin/sh
ifconfig wlan0 | grep 'RXbytes'
```

After building the shell script *wlan-stats.sh*, this script will be made executable by

chmod +x /tmp/wlan-stats.sh

In order to make it possible to start the execution by calling `/tmp/wlan-stats.sh` in the function `runScript()`.

The string `output` collects the response of that shell script for later output to the console. Figure 41 shows the output of the program *FileIO.ino*.

```
/*
  Write to file using FileIO classes.

  This sketch demonstrates how to write the file
  into the Yun file system.
  A shell script file is created in /tmp, and it
  is executed afterwards.

  created 7 June 2010
  by Cristian Maglie

  tested under v1.5.7
  by Claus Kuehnel 29-09-2014

  This example code is in the public domain.
*/

#include <FileIO.h>

void setup()
{
  // setup Bridge
  Bridge.begin();
```

```
  // initialize the Serial
  Serial.begin(9600);

  // wait for Serial port to connect.
  while(!Serial);
  Serial.println("File Write Script example");

  // setup File IO
  FileSystem.begin();

  // upload script used to gain network statis-
tics
  uploadScript();
}

void loop()
{
  // run stats script every five seconds
  runScript();
  delay(5000);
}

// this function creates a file into the Linux
// processor that contains a shell script
// to check the network traffic of the WiFi
// interface
void uploadScript()
{
  // write our shell script in /tmp
  // using /tmp stores, the script in RAM in this
  // way, we can preserve the limited amount of
  // FLASH erase/write cycles
  File script = FileSystem.open("/tmp/wlan-
stats.sh", FILE_WRITE);

  // shell script header
  script.print("#!/bin/sh\n");

  // shell commands:
  // ifconfig: is a command line utility for
  // controlling the network interfaces.
  // wlan0 is the interface we want to query
  // grep: search inside the output of the
  // ifconfig command the "RX bytes" keyword
  // and extract the line that contains it
```

```
  script.print("ifconfig wlan0 | grep 'RX
bytes'\n");
  script.close();  // close the file

  // make the script executable
  Process chmod;
  chmod.begin("chmod");      // chmod: change mode
  chmod.addParameter("+x"); // x stays for exec
  // path to the file to make it executable
  chmod.addParameter("/tmp/wlan-stats.sh");
  chmod.run();
}

// this function runs the script and reads the
// output data
void runScript()
{
  // run the script and show results on the Seri-
al
  Process myscript;
  myscript.begin("/tmp/wlan-stats.sh");
  myscript.run();

  String output = "";

  // read the output of the script
  while (myscript.available())
  {
    output += (char)myscript.read();
  }
  // remove the blank spaces at the beginning and
  // the ending of the string
  output.trim();
  Serial.println(output);
  Serial.flush();
}
```

Listing 18 Source code *FileIO.ino*

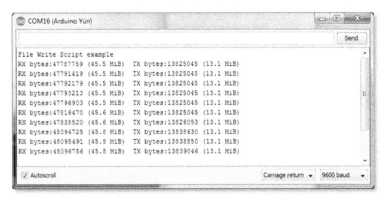

Figure 41 Output of program *FileIO.ino*

3.2.4 YunServer and YunClient

YunServer is the basic class for all calls of the Arduino Yún HTTP servers, while YunClient is the basic class for all calls of HTTP clients.

You can find the program sample *TemperaturWebPanel.ino* (Listing 19) in the Arduino Yún program samples for the Bridge library (".../Arduino1.5.7\libraries\Bridge\examples"), which is used for explanation here.

The program sample *TemperaturWebPanel.ino* measures the ambient temperature with a temperature sensor TMP36 and passes the data to the internal Arduino Yún web server. The used temperature sensor TMP36 is connected to the Arduino Yún according to Table 4.

Pin A0 serves as VCC, pin A1 captures the sensor signal and pin A2 serves as GND. The function `setup()` of the program *TemperatureWebPanel.ino* initializes these three pins.

On the highest layer of the connected SD card, we have to create the directory /arduino one layer below the directory /www.

Basically, we need an Arduino sketch and an HTML page (Listing 18). When you call the HTML page, this sends a request to the Arduino Yún web server, which will be answered by them.

```
<!DOCTYPE html>
<html>
  <head>
    <script type="text/javscript" src="zepto.min.js">
    </script>
```

```
    <script type="text/javascript">
      function refresh()
      {

$('#content').load('/arduino/temperature');
      }
    </script>
  </head>
  <body onload="setInterval(refresh, 1000);">
    <span id="content">0</span>
  </body>
</html>
```

Listing 18 HTML file *index.html*

Sending a request to the web server requires Javascript, which has not yet been used in this context. But we do not have to worry about it because using the Zepto library makes things easier.

Zepto is a compact JavaScript library for modern web browsers with an API largely compatible with jQuery. You can download *zepto.min.js* version v1.4 from the website http://zeptojs.com/ this time.

After the download, we copy the HTML files *index.html* (Listing 18) and *zepto.min.js* into the directory /www on the SD card created earlier.

Let us have a look at the Arduino program *TemperatureWebPanel.ino* (Listing 19).

At the beginning, the required libraries will be loaded. In this case, we need

```
#include<Bridge.h>
#include<YunServer.h>
#include<YunClient.h>
```

In the initialization, the YunServer object `server` and the variables `startString` and `hits` are initialized.

```
YunServer server;
String startString;
long hits=0;
```

In the function `setup()`, the serial communication and the Bridge are started. A bright LED (on IO13) shows the started Bridge. Thereafter, the configuration of the IO pins for connecting the temperature sensor TMP36 follows (see chapter 4.1.3). The server has to respond only to requests on the local host and is started. Finally, using `startTime`, an instance of Process is still produced, and by calling the Shell command `date` the current time retrieved and stored in the variable `startString`.

In function `loop()`, the YunClient object `client` is created first. If a new client is connected (`if(client)`), then the command sent can be read and output to the console after killing the white space using `trim()`.

If we receive the command "temperature", then the actual time is queried by the Shell command `date` again and saved in the variable `timeString`.

The measurement of ambient temperature is carried out by capturing the sensor output signal via pin A1, followed by a calculation of a voltage and temperature value in °C.

```
Int sensorValue=analogRead(A1);
//convert the reading to millivolts:
Float voltage=sensorValue*(5000/1024);
//convert the millivolts to temperature celsius
Float temperature=(voltage-500)/10;
```

Several instructions `client.print()` send these data back to the HTML page.

```
client.print("Current temperature:");
client.print(temperature);
client.println("degreesC");
```

If the request is answered by the web server, the client connection can be closed and used resources are freed. The variable `hits` is incremented finally, to get the number of queries.

Figure 42 shows the described query of the ambient temperature from a web browser.

```
/*
  Temperature web interface

  This example shows how to serve data from an analog input
  via the Arduino Yun's built-in web server using the
  Bridge library.

  The circuit:
  * TMP36 temperature sensor on analog pin A1
  * SD card attached to SD card slot of the Arduino Yun

  Prepare your SD card with an empty folder in the SD root
  named "arduino" and a subfolder of that named "www".
  This will ensure that the Yun will create a link
  to the SD to the "/mnt/sd" path.

  In this sketch folder is a basic webpage and a copy of
  zepto.js, a minimized version of jQuery. When you upload
  your sketch, these files will be placed in the
  /arduino/www/TemperatureWebPanel folder on your SD card.

  You can then go to
  http://arduino.local/sd/TemperatureWebPanel
  to see the output of this sketch.

  You can remove the SD card while the Linux and the
  sketch are running but be careful not to remove it while
  the system is writing to it.

  created  6 July 2013
  by Tom Igoe

  This example code is in the public domain.
*/

#include <Bridge.h>
#include <YunServer.h>
#include <YunClient.h>

// listen on default port 5555 ; the web server on the Yun
// will forward all the HTTP requests for us there.
YunServer server;
String startString;
long hits = 0;
```

```
void setup() {
  Serial.begin(9600);

  // bridge startup
  pinMode(13,OUTPUT);
  digitalWrite(13, LOW);
  Bridge.begin();
  digitalWrite(13, HIGH);

  // using A0 and A2 as vcc and gnd for the TMP36 sensor:
  pinMode(A0, OUTPUT);
  pinMode(A2, OUTPUT);
  digitalWrite(A0, HIGH);
  digitalWrite(A2, LOW);

  // listen for incoming connection only from localhost
  // (no one from the external network could connect)
  server.listenOnLocalhost();
  server.begin();

  // get the time that this sketch started:
  Process startTime;
  startTime.runShellCommand("date");
  while(startTime.available()) {
    char c = startTime.read();
    startString += c;
  }
}

void loop() {
  // get clients coming from server
  YunClient client = server.accept();

  // there is a new client?
  if (client) {
    digitalWrite(13, LOW);
    // read the command
    String command = client.readString();
    command.trim();          //kill whitespace
    Serial.println(command);
    // is "temperature" command?
    if (command == "temperature") {

      // get the time from the server:
      Process time;
```

```
    time.runShellCommand("date");
    String timeString = "";
    while(time.available()) {
      char c = time.read();
      timeString += c;
    }
    Serial.println(timeString);
    int sensorValue = analogRead(A1);
    // convert the reading to millivolts:
    float voltage = sensorValue * (5000/ 1024);
    // convert the millivolts to temperature Celsius:
    float temperature = (voltage - 500)/10;
    // print the temperature:
    client.println("Data from Arduino Yun Web-
server:");
    client.println("--------------------------
-----");
    client.print("Current time on the Yun: ");
    client.print(timeString);
    client.print("Current temperature: ");
    client.print(temperature);
    client.println(" degrees C");
    client.print("This sketch has been running
since ");
    client.print(startString);
    client.print("Hits so far: ");
    client.print(hits);
    digitalWrite(13, HIGH);
  }

  // Close connection and free resources.
  client.stop();
  hits++;
  }

  delay(50); // Poll every 50ms
}
```

Listing 19 Source code *TemperatureWebPanel.ino*

Figure 42 Temperature query

3.3 Temboo

Temboo is an interface to numerous applications accessible via cloud computing. Temboo provides over 2,000 Choreos named cloud-based and task-specific code components (https://temboo.com).

For Arduino Yún, I use here this Temboo technology for the use of web-based resources and services. Figure 43 shows the data flow from a sensor into the Temboo cloud. The flow direction can be orientated in reverse direction too (not shown here).

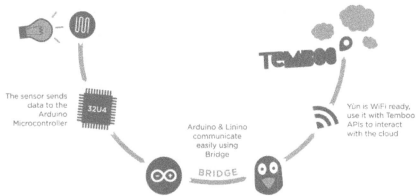

Figure 43 Data flow into the Temboo cloud

The ATmega32u4 captures sensor data and, via Bridge, they are sent to the Atheros AR9331. The Temboo client running on Atheros AR9331 transfers the data to the application in the Temboo cloud. Data can be stored, processed or queried there. For a query, data are transferred the same way back to the ATmega32u4 and, once there, can control IO pins or actors or are displayed on the monitor, for example. Figure 44 shows the distribution of the Temboo components.

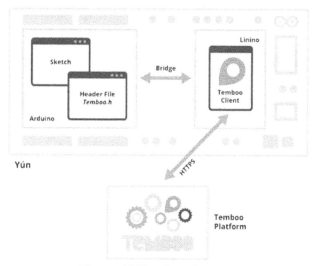

Figure 44 Temboo Components

Before we can use Temboo, we have to create a user account at https://temboo.com.

The Temboo login data (credentials) are stored in file *TembooAccount.h* (in Figure 44 named as *Temboo.h*) to isolate them from a **.ino* file. Due to the isolation of this non-public information from a **.ino* file, it is possible to publish Arduino sketches.

Over 2,000 Choreos of different areas like advertising, development, health, marketing, productivity, search, storage, weather, etc. are available for programming environments like iOS, Android, Java, PHP, Python, Ruby, Node.js, cURL and Arduino Yún.

For Google and Twitter applications, we again use a user account. For a lot of other Choreos or applications, it is the same. In Chapter 5.2, such access data can be notified.

Figure 45 shows the entry page for Arduino Yún with some applications (https://temboo.com/arduino/yun/).

Figure 45 Temboo entry page for Arduino Yún

It is important to install the Temboo library in the Arduino IDE v1.5.7. In the top-right edge of the Temboo entry page (see Figure 45), you can find a download button. I have downloaded the file *temboo-arduino-sdk-1.2.zip* and replaced the directory ...\Arduino 1.5.7\libraries\Temboo with that content.

After this update, I can explain the access to the Temboo cloud using some program samples.

In the first example, I will demonstrate how to test a chosen Choreo in the library already before an installation on an Arduino Yún.

3.3.1 Data in a Google Spreadsheet

In our next program sample, we want to save data captured by Arduino Yún in a Google Spreadsheet for further evaluation.

For this, I have created in Google Docs a table named Temboo Table, which shall consist of two columns that are labeled in the first line (Figure 46).

Figure 46 *TembooTable*

After logging onto the website https://temboo.com, we can call the AppendRow Choreo via Library > Google > Spreadsheet. The AppendRow Choreo transfers one line of data separated by a comma to the Google Spreadsheet.

Figure 47 shows how to test the AppendRow Choreo in the library. If the IoT mode is active ( ), then our Arduino Yún can be chosen as the target. In the field Input, we have to enter the Google login (password and username) at first. These data can be saved and called via "Insert Credentials" at any time. In the "Raw Data" field, we have to enter the data that should be transferred to the table separated by commas. In our case, this is a pair of values (here 700, 600). Finally, we have to enter the name of the table. One click on the button sends the prepared data via Temboo to the

Google Spreadsheet.

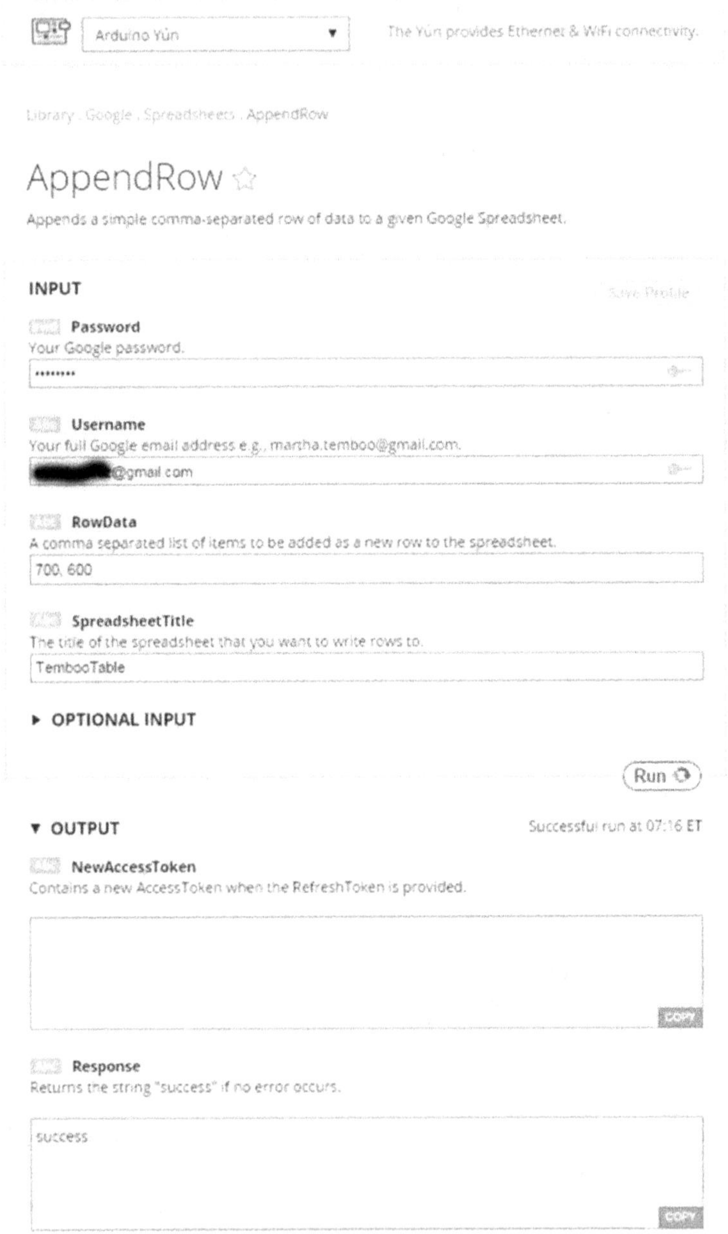

Arduino Yún ▼   The Yún provides Ethernet & WiFi connectivity.

Library . Google . Spreadsheets . AppendRow

AppendRow ☆

Appends a simple comma-separated row of data to a given Google Spreadsheet.

INPUT   Save Profile

Password
Your Google password.

....

Username
Your full Google email address e.g., martha.temboo@gmail.com.

@gmail.com

RowData
A comma separated list of items to be added as a new row to the spreadsheet.

700, 600

SpreadsheetTitle
The title of the spreadsheet that you want to write rows to.

TembooTable

▶ OPTIONAL INPUT

(Run ⟳)

▼ OUTPUT   Successful run at 07:16 ET

NewAccessToken
Contains a new AccessToken when the RefreshToken is provided.

COPY

Response
Returns the string "success" if no error occurs.

success

COPY

Figure 47 Test AppendRaw Choreo

The message "success" in the field Response signals a correct function. A better way is always to convince oneself on the success in the spreadsheet (Figure 48).

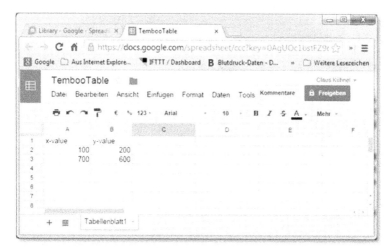

Figure 48 *TembooTable* **after LibraryTest**

Following this successful test, we can expect a correct function of this Choreo, download the generated Arduino code and take in a sketch (Listing 20).

```
#include <Bridge.h>
#include <Temboo.h>
#include "TembooAccount.h" // contains Temboo account
                           // information, as described below

// execution count, so this does not run forever
int numRuns = 1;
// maximum number of times the Choreo should be executed
int maxRuns = 10;

void setup() {
  Serial.begin(9600);

  // for debugging, wait until the serial console is connect-
ed.
  delay(4000);
  while(!Serial);
```

```
  Bridge.begin();
}

void loop() {
  if (numRuns <= maxRuns) {
    Serial.println("Running AppendRow - Run #" +
String(numRuns++));

    TembooChoreo AppendRowChoreo;

    // invoke the Temboo client
    AppendRowChoreo.begin();

    // set Temboo account credentials
    AppendRowChoreo.setAccountName(TEMBOO_ACCOUNT);
    AppendRowChoreo.setAppKeyName(TEMBOO_APP_KEY_NAME);
    AppendRowChoreo.setAppKey(TEMBOO_APP_KEY);

    // set profile to use for execution
    AppendRowChoreo.setProfile("CK");

    // set Choreo inputs
    AppendRowChoreo.addInput("RowData", "700, 600");
    AppendRowChoreo.addInput("SpreadsheetTitle", "TembooT-
able");

    // identify the Choreo to run
    AppendRowCho-
reo.setChoreo("/Library/Google/Spreadsheets/AppendRow");

    // run the Choreo; when results are available, print
them to serial
    AppendRowChoreo.run();

    while(AppendRowChoreo.available()) {
      char c = AppendRowChoreo.read();
      Serial.print(c);
    }
    AppendRowChoreo.close();
  }
```

```
Serial.println("Waiting...");
delay(30000); // wait 30 seconds between AppendRow calls
}
```

Listing 20 Downloaded source code

Additionally, the header file *TembooAccount.h* containing the Temboo Credentials is created. We have to copy this header file in that directory that contains our new sketch *.ino*. The Temboo Credentials are encapsulated in this file and separated from application program *.ino*.

In Figure 47, we have entered the Google login data. These data should also be hidden. Here are two options.

By the input of plain text, the specific code is generated in the following form. The Google password and username appear in plain text and were made unrecognizable by the characters "xxx" later. Password and username can be separated in a header that keeps them hidden in a transfer of the application program in the form of *.ino files.

```
//set choreo inputs
AppendRowChoreo.addInput("Password", "xxxxxxxx");
AppendRowChoreo.addInput("Username", "xxxx@gmail.com");
AppendRowChoreo.addInput("RowData", "700,600");
AppendRowChoreo.addInput("SpreadsheetTitle", "TembooTable");
```

A further option is the saving of the Credentials, which is used here. If these are inserted in the application later, then the Google credentials stand no longer in plain text in the code but are addressed by the given name (here CK).

```
// Set credential to use for execution
AppendRowChoreo.setCredential("CK");
```

```
//set choreo inputs
AppendRowChoreo.addInput("RowData", "700,600");
AppendRowChoreo.addInput("SpreadsheetTitle","TembooTable");
```

Listing 21 shows the source code of the program sample *TembooTable.ino*. Here, the second option is selected for the Google credentials.

```
#include <Bridge.h>
#include <Temboo.h>

// contains Temboo account information, as described below
#include "TembooAccount.h"
// execution count, so this doesn't run forever
int numRuns = 1;
// maximum number of times the Choreo should be executed
int maxRuns = 2;

void setup()
{
  Serial.begin(9600);

  // for debugging, wait until a serial console is connect-
ed.
  while(!Serial);
  Serial.println("Append Row into Google Spreadsheet via
Temboo");
  Bridge.begin();
}

void loop()
{
  if (numRuns <= maxRuns)
  {
    Serial.println("Running AppendRow - Run #" +
String(numRuns++));

    TembooChoreo AppendRowChoreo;

    // invoke the Temboo client
    AppendRowChoreo.begin();

    // set Temboo account credentials
    AppendRowChoreo.setAccountName(TEMBOO_ACCOUNT);
    AppendRowChoreo.setAppKeyName(TEMBOO_APP_KEY_NAME);
    AppendRowChoreo.setAppKey(TEMBOO_APP_KEY);

    // set credential to use for execution
    AppendRowChoreo.setCredential("CK");

    // set choreo inputs
    AppendRowChoreo.addInput("RowData", "1000, 1000");
```

```
AppendRowChoreo.addInput("SpreadsheetTitle", "TembooT-
able");

    // identify choreo to run
    AppendRowCho-
reo.setChoreo("/Library/Google/Spreadsheets/AppendRow");

    // run choreo; when results are available, print them to serial
    AppendRowChoreo.run();

    while(AppendRowChoreo.available())
    {
      char c = AppendRowChoreo.read();
      Serial.print(c);
    }
    AppendRowChoreo.close();
  }

  Serial.println("Waiting...");
  delay(10000);  // wait 10 seconds between AppendRow calls
}
```

Listing 21 Source code *TembooTable.ino*

Structurally, the program sample *TembooTable.ino* offers nothing that is essentially new. The variable maxRuns determines how many times the value pair is sent to the Google Spreadsheet. After the initialization of the AppendRow Choreo, the Temboo and the Google Credentials as well as the data (pair of values separated by comma) and the name of the table were provided to call the prepared Choreo at the end. The returned data is read in a loop and output afterwards. Figure 49 shows the monitored output.

Figure 49 Feedback for error-free transmission

By definition, two sets of data are sent to the Google Spreadsheet. Then the loop continues while outputting "Waiting ..." and a waiting time of 10 seconds without further activities endlessly. It is clear that this makes little sense in a real application. It is important here to know the building blocks that can be used effectively in a real application.

Finally, we want to be convinced again through success in the spreadsheet. Figure 50 shows the extensions of the table made by calling the AppendRow Choreo from Arduino Yún.

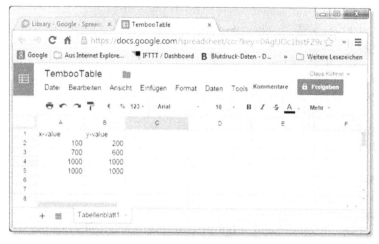

Figure 50 *TembooTable* **after Update**

3.3.2   Send Email through Google Mail

In Chapter 3.2.2, I had explained how to send an email by running a shell script.

Gmail is Google's free email service and, since mid-2012, the world's most popular one. We can use this service in a very simple manner via Temboo.

I have embedded sending an email into the program sample *StatusMonitor.ino* (Listing 22). The program monitors a digital input. If the state on input pIn changes, then the content of the variable state is changed too, and the output of the message "State is 0" or "State is 1"and toggling an LED follow.

Before explaining the email output controlled by the switch MAIL, we should study the extensive setup.

Arduino Yún and most other Arduino's have an LED connected to IO13, which we use here (pLED). The choice of IO9 as a digital input is arbitrary (pIn).

Function setup() initializes both IO pins. Setting IO9 to Hi (digitalWrite(pIn, HIGH)) enables the internal pull-up resistor so that for reading an open input, Hi always results.

Before the initialization of the serial port, IO9 is read and the state is saved in the variable old_state. The LED is switched on or off according to the state read.

In the main loop `loop()`, the string `msg` (`String msg = "State is"`) is declared as a variable and initialized. A query of IO9 follows.

But if the actual state differs from the old, the old state is overwritten (with the new state), a message is sent via the serial port and the LED is switched on or off according to the new state.

Now, our switch `MAIL` comes into play. If `MAIL` during the compilation is set to zero, then the source code between `#if` and `#end` will be not compiled.

Due to the conditional compiling, this code is not existent in the executable program. In this case, we can find in the lower part of the IDE the message: "Sketch uses 11,484 bytes (40%) of program storage space. Maximum is 28,672 bytes."

On the other hand, if our program sends an email when the state changes, then the switch `MAIL` must be set to one and the complete source code compiled. This was the original goal.

After a new compilation under this condition, we can find in the lower part of the IDE the message: "Sketch uses 14,026 bytes (48%) of program storage space. Maximum is 28,672 bytes." The email source code generated by Temboo includes 2,542 bytes.

The input of the credentials is done in the usual way. For the Google credentials, I chose the second option presented in Section 3.3.1 (stored credentials).

The structure of the email itself can be seen from the source code. It is possible to enter a subject so that these emails have the usual form. The email addresses of sender and receiver were made unrecognizable by the characters xxxx. This needs to be adjusted before compiling the data desired by the user.

After a waiting period of one second, the query of IO9 and all following activities are repeated.

Figure 51 shows the serial output captured by the monitor after activation of a contact or sensor connected to IO9. Figure 52 shows a received email after changing the state to zero on pin IO9.

```
// Title      : Status Monitor for digital Input
// Author     : Claus Kühnel
// Date       : 2013-09-30
// Id         : StatusMonitor.ino
// Version    : 1.5.7
// Micro      : Arduino Yún
//
// DISCLAIMER:
// The author is in no way responsible for any problems or
// damage caused by using this code. Use at your own risk.
//
// LICENSE:
// This code is distributed under the GNU Public License,
// which can be found at
// http://www.gnu.org/licenses/gpl.txt
//
// -----------------------------------------------------------

#include <Bridge.h>
#include <Temboo.h>

// contains Temboo account information, as described below
#include "TembooAccount.h"

#define MAIL 1              // set 0 to avoid mailing

// Pin 13 has an LED connected on most Arduino boards.
const int pLed = 13;
const int pIn = 9;

boolean old_state;
boolean state;

void setup()
{
  // initialize the digital IO pins.
  pinMode(pLed, OUTPUT);
  pinMode(pIn, INPUT);
  digitalWrite(pIn, HIGH);       //Pull-up active
  old_state = digitalRead(pIn);
  digitalWrite(pLed, old_state);

  // initialize serial port
  Serial.begin(9600);
  delay(4000);
```

```
  while(!Serial);
  Serial.println("Monitoring state on IO9...");
  Serial.print("State after initialization is ");
  Serial.println(old_state);
  Bridge.begin();
}

// the loop routine runs over and over again forever:
void loop()
{
  String msg = "State is ";

  state = digitalRead(pIn);
  if (state != old_state)
  {
    old_state = state;
    digitalWrite(pLed, state);
    Serial.println(msg + state);

    #if (MAIL)
    {
      TembooChoreo SendEmailChoreo;

      // invoke the Temboo client
      SendEmailChoreo.begin();

      // set Temboo account credentials
      SendEmailChoreo.setAccountName(TEMBOO_ACCOUNT);
      SendEmailChoreo.setAppKeyName(TEMBOO_APP_KEY_NAME);
      SendEmailChoreo.setAppKey(TEMBOO_APP_KEY);

      // set credential to use for execution
      SendEmailChoreo.setCredential("CK");

      // set choreo inputs
      SendEmailChoreo.addInput("MessageBody", msg + state);
      SendEmailChoreo.addInput("Subject", "IO9 State");
      SendEmailChoreo.addInput("FromAddress",
"xxxx@gmail.com");
      SendEmailChoreo.addInput("ToAddress",
"xxxx@xxxx.ch");

      // identify choreo to run
      SendEmailCho-
reo.setChoreo("/Library/Google/Gmail/SendEmail");
```

```
    // run choreo; when results are available, print them to serial
    SendEmailChoreo.run();

    while(SendEmailChoreo.available()) {
      char c = SendEmailChoreo.read();
      Serial.print(c);
    }
    SendEmailChoreo.close();
  }
  #endif
  delay(1000);
 }
}
```

Listing 22 Source code *StatusMonitor.ino*

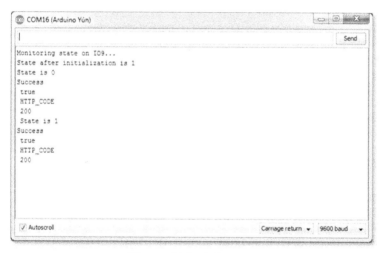

Figure 51 Serial output

Figure 52 Received email

3.3.3　Twitter

Twitter is a digital application for micro-blogging that is used to distribute short text messages (tweets) via the internet. Tweets sent may have a maximum of 140 characters.

To create such tweets, the user must have a Twitter account. Reading of tweets is possible without registration. Tweets are displayed in the first place to the followers of a user. By using hashtags (#) or links (URL), a wider audience can also be reached.

We want to use Twitter here for sending status messages. In addition to registration on Temboo, we need further registration on Twitter at https://twitter.com/signup.

Afterward, we have to create a new application on https://dev.twitter.com/apps to get the Twitter ConsumerKey and ConsumerSecret data. On the Temboo website we find under the heading Twitter >Tweets, the StatusesUpdate that we will use for sending the tweet.

Figure 53 shows the preparation of a tweet on the Temboo website. AccessToken and AccessTokenSecret are the access data of Temboo and were stored in the credentials and included here. ConsumerKey and ConsumerSecret are the access data for the Twitter app in question.

Now, we have to enter the message to be sent—the tweet—into the box Status Update.

A click to the `Run ○` field sends the prepared data from the

Temboo website to the TwitterStatusesUpdate Choreo. In the output box below, the data received from Twitter can be viewed. More interesting here is the message "Successful run at 09:26 ET." The message confirms a successful operation.

To check the result, we open the Twitter account from any PC and can look for that tweet. The tweet sent is readable via Twitter (Figure 54).

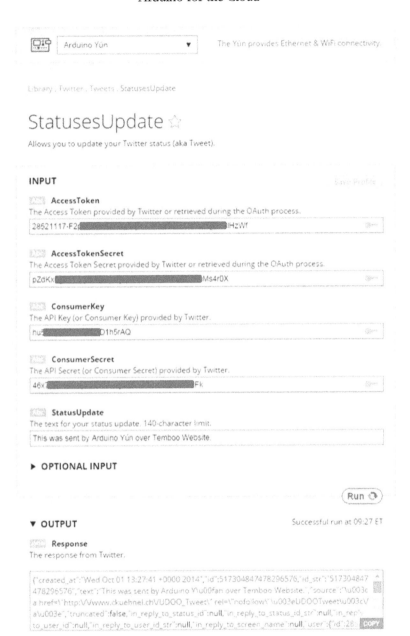

Figure 53 Preparing a tweet on the Temboo website

Figure 54 Tweet sent from the Temboo website

To create the tweet not on the Temboo website but on the Arduino Yún, just download the generated code. The downloaded file *sketch_statusesupdate.zip* contains both *sketch_statusesupdate.ino* and *TembooAccout.h*, including the Temboo credentials.

I have renamed the first file as *TembooTweet.ino* and copied both files into the folder TembooTweet. We can now open the .ino file in the Arduino IDE and make adaptations at one point or another before download. Listing 23 shows the source code *TembooTweet.ino*. Lines included or edited afterward are marked in bold.

```
#include <Bridge.h>
#include <Temboo.h>

// contains Temboo account information, as described below
#include "TembooAccount.h"

// Pin 13 has an LED connected on most Arduino boards.
const int led = 13;

// Execution count, so this doesn't run forever
int numRuns = 1;
// Maximum number of times the Choreo should be executed
int maxRuns = 2;

void setup()
{
  Serial.begin(9600);

  // For debugging, wait until the serial console is connected.
  delay(4000);
  while(!Serial);
  Serial.println("Sending status info to Twitter via Tem-
boo");
  Bridge.begin();
}

void loop()
```

```
{
  if (numRuns <= maxRuns)
  {
    Serial.println("Running StatusesUpdate - Run #" +
String(numRuns++));

    TembooChoreo StatusesUpdateChoreo;

    // Invoke the Temboo client
    StatusesUpdateChoreo.begin();

    // Set Temboo account credentials
    StatusesUpdateChoreo.setAccountName(TEMBOO_ACCOUNT);
    StatusesUpdateChoreo.setAppKeyName(TEMBOO_APP_KEY_NAME);
    StatusesUpdateChoreo.setAppKey(TEMBOO_APP_KEY);

    // Set profile to use for execution
    StatusesUpdateChoreo.setProfile("UDOOTweet");

    // Set Choreo inputs
    StatusesUpdateChoreo.addInput("StatusUpdate", "This #Ar-
duino #Yun is running " + String(millis()) + " ms.");

    // Identify the Choreo to run
    StatusesUpdate-
Choreo.setChoreo("/Library/Twitter/Tweets/StatusesUpdate");

    // Run the Choreo; when results are available, print them to serial
    StatusesUpdateChoreo.run();

    while(StatusesUpdateChoreo.available())
    {
      char c = StatusesUpdateChoreo.read();
      Serial.print(c);
    }
    StatusesUpdateChoreo.close();
  }

  Serial.println("Waiting...");

for (int i = 0; i < 6; i++)
{
  for (int j = 0; j < 10; j++)
  {
    // turn the LED on (HIGH is the voltage level)
```

```
    digitalWrite(led, HIGH);
    delay(20); // wait for a second
    // turn the LED off by making the voltage LOW
    digitalWrite(led, LOW);
    delay(980); // wait for a second
  }
  Serial.write("*");
 }
 Serial.println();
}
```

Listing 23 Source code *TembooTweet.ino*

The structure of the program sample *TembooTweet.ino* can be compared to the previous Temboo examples. The Temboo credentials are stored in the header file *TembooAccount.h*.

As the LED connected to IO13 is used here, the constant `led` is initialized here.

I have reduced the number of tweets to two (`maxRuns=2`), so as not to unnecessarily send many virtually identical tweets.

Sending the first tweet is commented on by the message "RunningStatusesUpdate-Run1", before the choreo in question is called. It starts by sending the Temboo account credentials followed by the Twitter credentials stored under `UDOOTweet`. Thereafter, the tweet with the content "This #Arduino #Yun is running xxx ms." follows. The words "Arduino" and "Yun" have a preceding character "#", which highlights these words in the tweet (Figure 56).

The program sample reads the characters received from Choreo and outputs these to the console (monitor). Figure 55 shows the terminal output.

The output "Waiting…" signals the beginning of a waiting period of 60 seconds. Over this waiting period, the LED connected to IO13 blinks once a second and the character "*" is output every 10 seconds.

Since only two tweets in a one-minute interval are sent, in the following iterations of the loop, only the waiting time with its outputs is processed.

Figure 55 Terminal output of *TembooTweet.ino*

Figure 56 Tweets inTwitter

3.3.4 Temboo Device Coder

The creation of cloud-based applications had already been greatly simplified through support from Temboo.

But Temboo now shows the Temboo Device Coder as a way to generate complete programs without writing a single line of code. I will illustrate this with a simple example here.

Temboo has replaced the Device Coder with a new feature that is called "Conditions". Sketches generated previously with the Device coder should continue to work as they did.

The new feature offers similar functionality but allows you to generate sketches with input/output triggers for any Choreo in the library. You can test this out by turning on IoT Mode when browsing Choreos in the library. For more information about using the condition triggers, have a look to https://temboo.com/conditions.

The Temboo Device Coder we can access via the Temboo website with the URL https://temboo.com/library/Library/Devices/. Figure 57 shows the initial screen for selecting a sensor whose data should trigger an action that is yet to be defined.

HOW IT WORKS

Figure 57 Temboo Device Coder

If we choose the Arduino Yún here, then we obtain the following sensor type for selection (Figure 58).

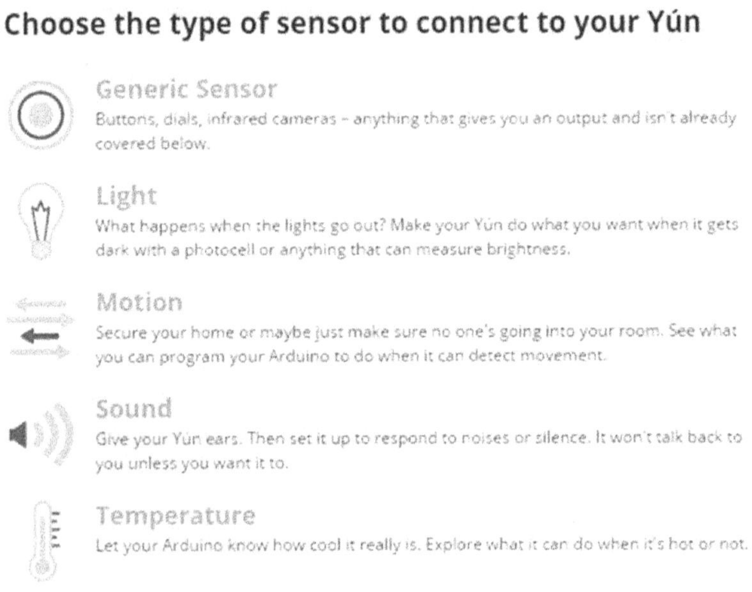

Choose the type of sensor to connect to your Yún

Generic Sensor

Buttons, dials, infrared cameras – anything that gives you an output and isn't already covered below.

Light

What happens when the lights go out? Make your Yún do what you want when it gets dark with a photocell or anything that can measure brightness.

Motion

Secure your home or maybe just make sure no one's going into your room. See what you can program your Arduino to do when it can detect movement.

Sound

Give your Yún ears. Then set it up to respond to noises or silence. It won't talk back to you unless you want it to.

Temperature

Let your Arduino know how cool it really is. Explore what it can do when it's hot or not.

Figure 58 Sensor selection

For the sensors here, it is always assumed that an analog output is present. The output voltage range is adjusted to the 5V input voltage range of the internal AD converter. If you have another analog voltage range or even a digital sensor, then you must yourself carry out the necessary adjustments in the generated code.

After selecting the desired sensor, a selection of the relevant application (Figure 59) appears. Depending on the status of the selected sensor, we can send an email, feed a MySQL database with data, call or send a text message, make an entry in a Google Spreadsheet or send an Amazon SQS message.

Choose what you want to do with a generic sensor

Email
Set your Yún up to send an email whenever it's triggered by a sensor reading that you set.

MySQL
Get your Yún to log particular sensor readings to a MySQL database.

Phone
Make your Yún call your phone. Then control it with your keypad!

SMS
Receive an SMS alert from your Yún when the sensor is triggered.

Spreadsheet
Have your Yún record sensor values to a Google Spreadsheet.

SQS
Program your Yún to send Amazon SQS messages in response to sensor readings.

Figure 59 Selection of an application

In our program sample, I would like to receive an SMS at a given sensor output signal. Therefore, it is necessary to seek an appropriate provider. I have tried a test account with Twilio (https://www.twilio.com/). Twilio provides SMS and voice APIs that can be used here.

Figure 60 shows how the actions to be triggered at a pre-settable sensor value can be defined.

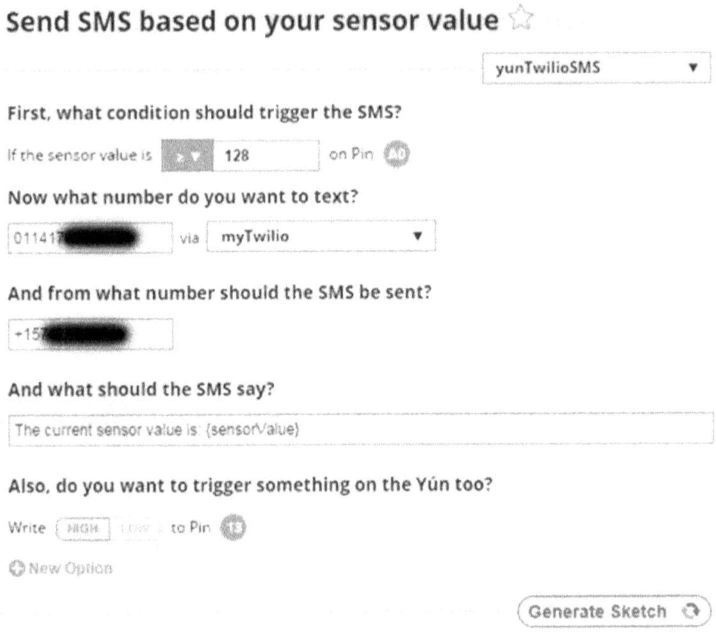

Send SMS based on your sensor value ☆

yunTwilioSMS ▼

First, what condition should trigger the SMS?

If the sensor value is [▲▼] 128 on Pin (A0)

Now what number do you want to text?

01141▓▓▓ via | myTwilio ▼

And from what number should the SMS be sent?

+15▓▓▓

And what should the SMS say?

The current sensor value is: {sensorValue}

Also, do you want to trigger something on the Yún too?

Write [HIGH | LOW] to Pin (13)

⊕ New Option

(Generate Sketch ↻)

Figure 60 Definition of an action to be triggered

We want to send an SMS via Twilio to the entered phone number when a sensor value of 128 at pin A0 is exceeded. The upper number is the phone number of the recipient. Since it will be called from the US, it has to be entered in the form 01141 for Switzerland and 01149 for Germany. The lower number is the US phone number assigned to the Twilio account. The actual numbers have been defaced here.

The outgoing message is entered in the field "And what should the SMS say?" Furthermore, actions on the Arduino Yún can be defined. Here, it was agreed that upon receipt of an SMS, the LED connected to IO13 is turned on.

Pressing the button (Generate Sketch ↻) generates the complete source code for the program sample *sketch_sms.ino* according to Listing 24. The lines marked in bold were changed or included afterward.

```
#include <Bridge.h>
#include <Temboo.h>
#include "TembooAccount.h" // contains Temboo account infor-
mation
// the number of times to trigger the action if the condition is met.
// we limit this so you won't use all of your Temboo calls while test-
ing.
int maxCalls = 2;

// the number of times this Choreo has been run so far in this sketch.
int calls = 0;

void setup()
{
  Serial.begin(9600);

  // for debugging, wait until the serial console is connected.
  delay(4000);
  while(!Serial);
  Serial.println("Sending SMS triggered by sensor value");
  Bridge.begin();

  // initialize pins
  pinMode(A0, INPUT);
  pinMode(13, OUTPUT);

  Serial.println("Setup complete.\n");
}

void loop()
{
  int sensorValue = analogRead(A0);

  Serial.println("Sensor: " + String(sensorValue));

  if (sensorValue >= 128)
  {
    if (calls < maxCalls)
    {
      Serial.println("\nTriggered! Calling Li-
brary/Twilio/SMSMessages/SendSMS...");

      runSendSMS(sensorValue);
      digitalWrite(13, HIGH);
      calls++;
```

```
     }
   else
   {
     Serial.println("\nTriggered! Skipping action to save
Temboo calls during testing.");
       Serial.println("You can adjust or remove the
calls/maxCalls if() statement to change this behavior.\n");
     }
   }
   delay(1000);
}

void runSendSMS(int sensorValue)
{
   TembooChoreo SendSMSChoreo;

   // invoke the Temboo client
   SendSMSChoreo.begin();

   // set Temboo account credentials
   SendSMSChoreo.setAccountName(TEMBOO_ACCOUNT);
   SendSMSChoreo.setAppKeyName(TEMBOO_APP_KEY_NAME);
   SendSMSChoreo.setAppKey(TEMBOO_APP_KEY);

   // set profile to use for execution
   SendSMSChoreo.setProfile("yunTwilioSMS");

   // set Choreo inputs
   String BodyValue = String("The current sensor value is: ")
+ String(sensorValue);
   SendSMSChoreo.addInput("Body", BodyValue);

   // identify the Choreo to run
   SendSMSCho-
reo.setChoreo("/Library/Twilio/SMSMessages/SendSMS");

   // run the Choreo
   unsigned int returnCode = SendSMSChoreo.run();

   // a return code of zero means everything worked
   if (returnCode == 0)
   {
     Serial.println("Done!\n");
   }
   else
```

```
{
    // a non-zero return code means there was an error
    // read and print the error message
    while (SendSMSChoreo.available())
    {
        char c = SendSMSChoreo.read();
        Serial.print(c);
    }
    Serial.println();
}

SendSMSChoreo.close();
}
```

Listing 24 Source code *sketch_sms.ino*

Figure 61 shows the output of the program *sketch_sms.ino*. After setup, the sensor value is still zero but increases later. Nothing happens for a value of 87, but when it reaches the value 128, the test condition (>= 128) is satisfied and the SMS is triggered. After this event, the value is zero and no other triggers follow. The received SMS from your phone is shown in Figure 62.

Figure 61 Output of program *sketch_sms.ino*

Figure 62 Received SMS

4   Linux Device AtherosAR9331

This section addresses the Atheros AR9331 as an independent Linux device. Thus, the execution of Shell, Lua or Python scripts created on the Atheros AR9331 can be started by activities on the ATmega32u4 and they can retrieve data from ATmega32u4.

A number of Linux tools are needed for the autonomous operation of the Atheros AR9331 as an independent Linux device to access the file system, to be able to install applications, etc. I present some tools that are commonly used in other Linux systems as well.

4.1.1   SSH Access

SSH (secure shell protocol) provides the ability to install a secure connection for exchanging data between two computers.

An SSH server is included in the Linino (OpenWRT) distribution already. From the development PC installed in the network the Arduino Yún can be accessed using the PuTTY SSH client, for example.

PuTTY is a free Telnet/SSH client and can be downloaded from http://www.chiark.greenend.org.uk/~sgtatham/putty/ for installation on the development PC afterward.

Figure 63 shows the configuration of PuTTY to access the Arduino Yún. For this purpose, the IP address 192.168.1.4 (used here) and the specified SSH port 22 must be entered. To be sure, save this configuration under an appropriate name.

If you open the desired connection, then the Arduino Yún responds with its login. By default, you login as user root with the Arduino Yún password assigned during configuration and get the command-line interface for further input. Figure 64 shows the access to the command line via PuTTY for Arduino Yún. Figure 65 uses the same access to the Dragino Yún shield.

Please remember that all used IP addresses are specific for your network and will differ from the addresses used here. See Chapter 2.7 for details.

Figure 63 *PuTTY* configuration

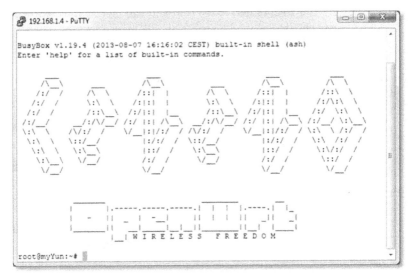

Figure 64 Arduino Yún—access by *PuTTY*

Figure 65 Dragino Yún shield—access by *PuTTY*

4.1.2   SCP Access

To get access from the network to the file system of the Arduino Yún, we use an SCP/FTP client.

WinSCP is a graphic open-source SFTP and FTP client for Windows, which supports the SCP protocol too. WinSCP offers a save data and file transfer feature between different computers and can be downloaded from the website http://winscp.net/eng/index.php.

Figure 66 shows the Arduino Yún login, while Figure 67 shows the access data itself.

The screenshots of the WinSCP contain some German text. The WinSCP version downloaded from the URL mentioned above is the English version. I believe you will have no problems with the interpretation of different layouts.

In addition to the IP address and port, the user root and the password specified at configuration must be set here. This configuration I have saved as myYun@192.168.1.4, so the next login is greatly simplified.

Figure 66 WinSCP login

Figure 67 WinSCP configuration

If you can log in, then the window shown in Figure 68 opens. On the right side, you can see the /root directory of the Arduino Yún and on the left a directory with source code from my project directory. In the bottom line, you can see the available commands through which all file transfers can be done.

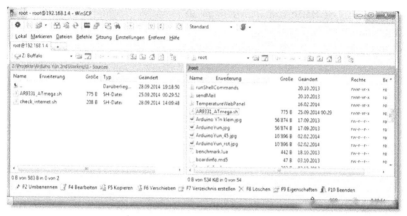

Figure 68 Access to directory/root

4.1.3   Package Manager OPKG

With a package manager in a Linux system, you can install, uninstall, and update software from the command line. So, much of the administrative work can be automated easily.

In the Linux-Wiki (http://linuxwiki.de/PaketManager), a package manager is called in as the usher of a distribution. Its tasks include:

- Installation of software packages
- Complete uninstallation of software packages
- Recognition of dependencies among packages
- Verification of software packages (signature check)
- Querying the package manager database (e.g. "what all is installed?")

Under OpenWRT, a package manager is available with *OPKG*, which can download OpenWRT software packages from local repositories or from the Internet and install them on your system.

OPKG is a complete package manager for the root file system including ways to install kernel modules and drivers and resolve dependencies of packages with each other.

The OpenWRT-Wiki describes the available *OPKG* commands in detail (http://wiki.openwrt.org/doc/techref/opkg).

I will explain the installation of a software package with the installation of Basic Calculator *bc* as an example. In addition to the installation of *bc*, I will also show the use of *bc* through several examples in Figure 69, but which are not considered further in detail.

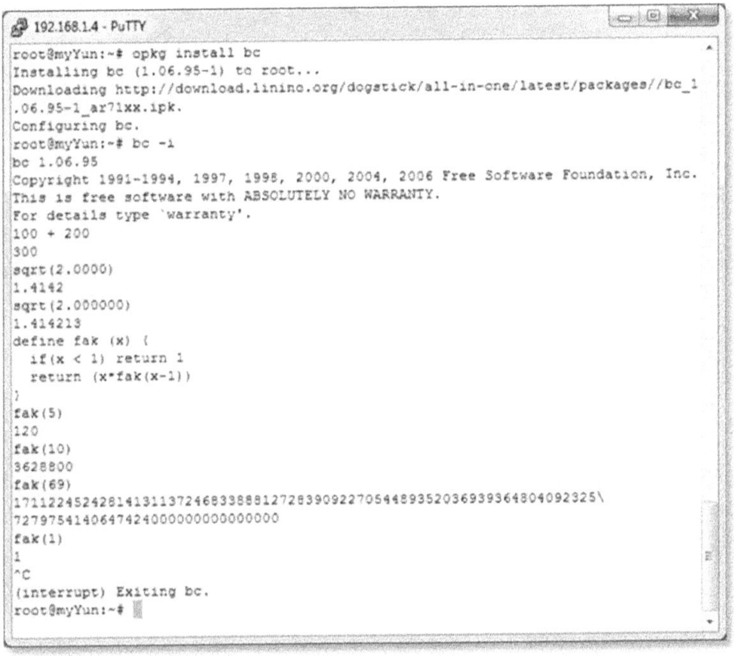

Figure 69 Installation and usage of Basic Calculator *bc*

You can also reach the package manager using the LuCI web interface, which is considered in detail in the following section (Figure 70).

Figure 70 Package manager in LuCI web interface

4.1.4   LuCI Web Interface

The original reason for the development of LuCI was the lack of a clear, clean, extensible and easy-to-maintain web interface for embedded systems.

LuCI uses the Lua scripting language and separates the interface into logical components, models and views to ensure better performance, smaller size, lower run times and easier maintainability.

At this point, the router assigned the IP address 192.168.1.4 to my Arduino. This IP address we now use to test accessing the Arduino from the developer's PC. Some screenshots explain the usage of the LuCI web interface.

To call the LuCI web interface, we have to enter the IP address in the web browser on the developer's PC. After entering the password at login, the Arduino web panel opens (Figure 71).

I have connected my Arduino Yún via WLAN; therefore, this interface is marked as "connected". Pressing the button CONFIGURE switches to the configuration from Chapter 2.7 (Figure 72).

Figure 71 Arduino web panel

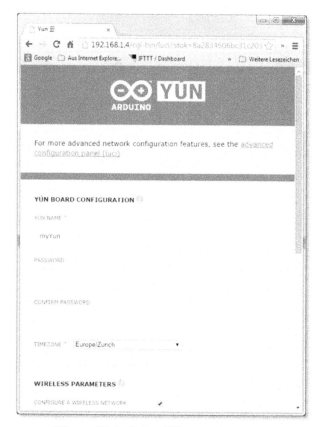

Figure 72 Arduino Yún configuration

From the Arduino web panel, we call the LuCI web interface finally by clicking the link "advanced configuration panel (luci)". Figure 73 shows the opening Status window, which can be reached via Status>Overview later again.

Figure 73 LuCI—status overview

We can see data that can be queried by commands from the command line (CLI) like uname -a, uptime, free et al.

Via the menu item Status>Realtime Graphs, some system states can be queried for visualizing their time profile.

Figure 74 shows the CPU load in a window over two minutes with an update rate of three seconds. The three curves illustrated show the course of the mean values over one minute, five minutes, or 15 minutes.

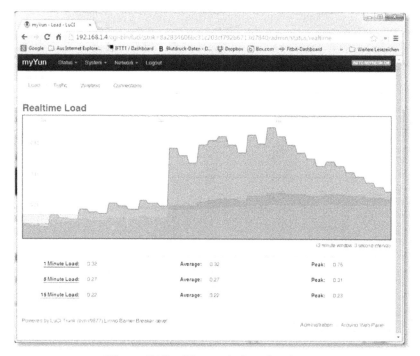

Figure 74 LuCI—real-time load

Figure 75 shows the throughput of the WLAN interface for incoming and outgoing data.

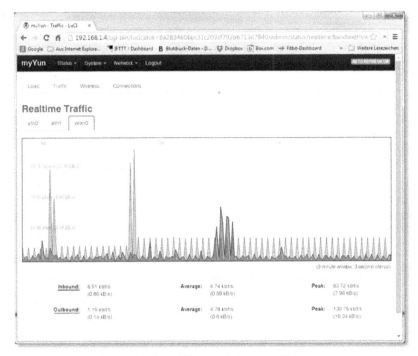

Figure 75 LuCI—real-time traffic

Via the menu item Network>Diagnostics we can run the tools *Ping, Traceroute,* and *Nslookup.* In Figure 76, it has been attempted to achieve the URL openwrt.org over the ping command. The answer comes from the CLI as usual and is displayed in the output field. In the communication, no data packet was lost and the average response time is approximately 52 milliseconds.

Via the menu item System>Scheduled Tasks, the Cron tab of the system will be shown (Figure 77) and can be changed. In Chapter 4.2.1.5, I will explain Cron jobs in detail. Therefore, at this point, the reference to the Cron tab should suffice.

Arduino for the Cloud

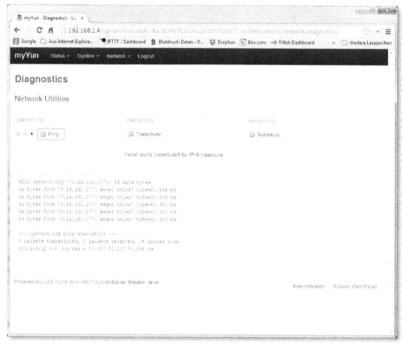

Figure 76 LuCI—network diagnostics

141

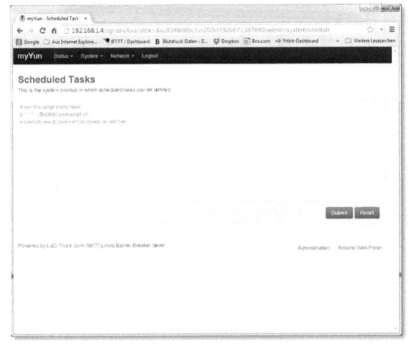

Figure 77 LuCI—scheduled tasks

LuCI consists of a variety of Lua modules that can be modified to extend the functionality of LuCI or supplemented by new modules. Figure 78 shows where these modules can be found. To extend these modules, I must refer to the corresponding OpenWRT documentation at the URL http://wiki.openwrt.org/doc/devel/luci.

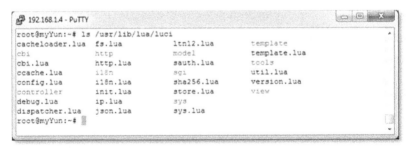

Figure 78 LuCI—Lua module

4.1.5 Editor *Nano*

For instituting changes to the source code of programs, we need an editor. Under Linino (OpenWRT), the editor *vi* is available.

The editor *vi* is a UNIX standard. For anyone who uses *vi* only occasionally, it is rather tedious. A simple alternative is the editor *nano* which can be installed by the command

```
# opkg install nano
```

and started by

```
# nano boardinfo.sh
```

to edit the file *boardinfo.sh*, for example. Figure 79 shows the opened file *boardinfo.sh*, which will be explained in the context of further Linux applications (chapter4.2.1.1).

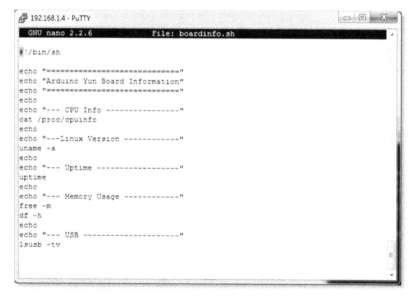

Figure 79 Editing with *nano*

4.1.6 File Manager Midnight Commander

GNU Midnight Commander is a file manager that can copy, move and delete files and folders. In addition, you can search for files and commands can be executed in a sub-shell. Viewer and editor are included in the *GNU Midnight Commander* (http://www.midnight-commander.org/).

The *GNU Midnight Commander* is not included in the basic installation on the Arduino Yún and has to be installed afterward.

Entering

```
# opkg install mc
```

calls the installation package. After a successful installation, the *GNU Midnight Commander* can be started by entering

```
# mc
```

and an user interface appears that is still familiar to one or the other of the DOS times (Figure 80).

Figure 80 *GNU Midnight Commander mc*

GNU Midnight Commander supports all function keys and the mouse, so that fairly comfortable work is possible.

4.1.7 Data Transfer by *cURL*

Using *cURL* (client for URLs), a command-line program to transfer files in computer networks, such tasks can be very effectively addressed.

The program *cURL* supports numerous protocols such as HTTP, HTTPS, FTPS, LDAP, RTMP and FTP and is available under the open MIT license.

It is ported to several operating systems and is available under Linino too (http://en.wikipedia.org/wiki/CURL). Figure 81 shows the query of the *cURL* version installed. In this installation, we have *cURL* in v ersion 7.29.0.

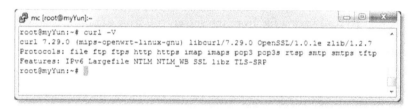

Figure 81 Query of *cURL* Version

cURL has several command-line options. Only a few can be presented here. I will explain the usage of *cURL* on the basis of a file upload into the cloud storage *ownCloud* and a file download of this file.

ownCloud provides location-independent data storage and, unlike commercial storage services, can be installed on a private server at no additional cost. If you are unwilling to entrust your personal data to a cloud provider, then this type of installation is an alternative worth considering.

Arvixe WebHosting (http://arvixe.com) offers a free account for *ownCloud* users with 1 GB storage, which is a suitable environment for our tests. Further providers can be found under http://owncloud.org/providers/.

If you have an account at Arvixe, for example, you get access immediately. For FTP, you get access with:

Host:	user.owncloud.arvixe.com
FTP Username:	user

FTP Password: passwd

FTP username user and password passwd are the entry data agreed upon at registration and must be adapted to its own conditions here (see Chapter 5.2, too).

To upload a file to a file server, you can now proceed as follows:

```
# curl -T file -u user:passwd ftp://ftp.upload.com/
```

The file named *file* is sent via FTP to the server ftp.upload.com. In our case, the server address is user.owncloud.arvixe.com.

If you want to attach the file content to an existing file, the call must be modified as follows:

```
# curl -T file -u user:passwd -a ftp://ftp.upload.com/
```

To read back a file from the server, you have to do the following call:

```
# curl -u user:passwd ftp://ftp.upload.com/text.txt
```

Figure 82 presents the steps described with reference to a screenshot. First, I created a text file *test.txt* with the content "Das ist Text in einem File" on Arduino Yún.

The first *cURL* command transfers the created file *test.txt* to user.owncloud.arvixe.com. The subsequent log shows the upload progress and the upload time (one second).

The next *cURL* command downloads the file *test.txt* from server address user.owncloud.arvixe.com and visualizes it via console (stdout).

A further *cURL* command transfers the file *test.txt* to user.owncloud.arvixe.com and appends it to the existing file *test.txt* there (-a). The subsequent log shows the upload progress and the upload time (one second) again.

The last *cURL* command downloads the file *test.txt* again from user.owncloud.arvixe.com and shows its content via console (stdout). You can now see the appended file content.

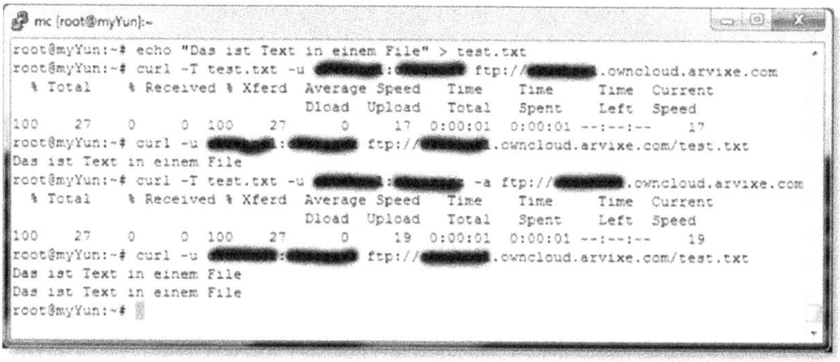

Figure 82 File transfer using *cURL*

Through these explanations, we have a way of executing file transfers to the external memory, which can help us to overcome the limited memory resources of the Arduino Yún effectively.

Sending an email from the command line shows a further possibility of using cURL (Listing 25).

```
#!/bin/sh

echo "Sending mail via cURL"
curl --url "smtps://smtp.gmail.com:465" --ssl-reqd --user
"xxxx@gmail.com:xxxx" --insecure
--mail-from "xxxx@gmail.com" --mail-rcpt "xxxx@gmx.ch" -T
/home/ubuntu/mail.txt
echo "Mail sent."
```

Listing 25 Shell script *sendmail.sh*

Initiated by the so-called "shebang," this instructs the operating system to run the script using the Bourne shell *sh*, and a simple output by command echo follows. The call of *cURL* with a long list of parameters comes next. Pay attention, this list of parameters needs to be listed in the editor in one row!

In this context, the codes mean the following:

--url	The URL of Google's mail servers, including port
--ssl-regd	Usage of SSL/TLS for connecting
--user	User and password of the Google account
--insecure	Use of "insecure" SSL connection
--mail-from	eMail address of transmitter
--mail-rcpt	eMail address of recipient
--upload-file	eMail content

Listing 25 has shown that the Google mail server was used for sending the email. The Google username, password and email addresses were defaced by the characters xxxx and must be changed to the conditions of the user. The file *mail.txt* contains the text of the email to be sent. The end of the script forms a single echo again.

Figure 83 shows the content of the file to be sent by calling the command cat mail.txt, followed by calling the shell script by ./sendmail.sh.

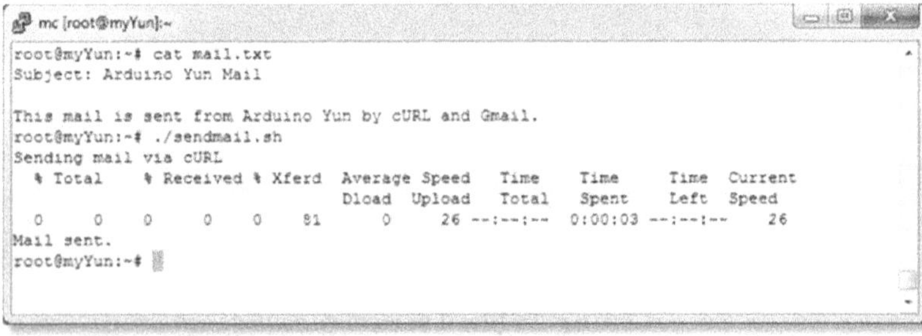

Figure 83 Sending email using *cURL*

After calling the shell script ./sendmail.sh, the first output with echo follows before we can see the communication protocol of the *cURL* command. 81 bytes will be sent via a transmission rate of 26 bytes/second and approximately three-second durations. The end of the script is signaled by the output "Mail sent."

cURL offers a good base to take advantage of other web services, which can be shown, for example, with *Temboo*. However, we used the Bridge library (Chapter 3.3).

148

To enhance the usage of *cURL*, refer to the website http://curl.haxx.se/. This also contains a comprehensive manual. Illustrative examples are in [8] and [9], for example.

4.1.8 Process Monitor *htop*

There are various standard programs for viewing the system performance. One of these standard programs is *top*. This program offers fast viewing of the processes currently running and the system load. This is usually sufficient. However, it does not offer a good overview.

htop offers the ability to scroll through the list of processes, including the ability to send certain signals to processes quickly and easily (Figure **84**).

It also offers the option of displaying process trees (which process was started by which process), and is far more customizable and clear than *top* (http://hisham.hm/htop/). Through mouse support, *htop* is also more convenient for operating compared to *top*.

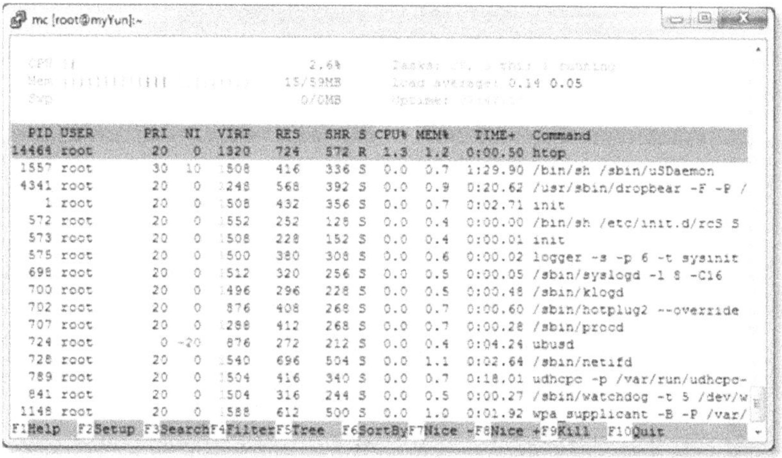

Figure 84 **Process Monitor** *htop*

4.2 Programming

To create your own application programs with Arduino Yún, Linino (OpenWRT) has some powerful tools onboard.

Above all, calling the shell itself and Python are preferred by many users. The LuCI web interface (chapter 4.1.4) was written in Lua; hence, Lua is also briefly mentioned here.

Figure 85 shows several development tools and their versions available under Linino (OpenWRT) for the Arduino Yún:

- Ash Shell as part of BusyBox version 1.19.4
- Bash in version 4.2.28 (must be installed additionally)
- Python in version 2.7.3
- Lua in version 5.1.5

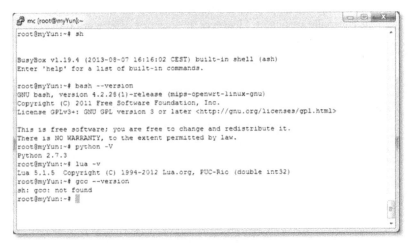

Figure 85 Development tools and their versions

BusyBox is referred as the Swiss army knife of embedded Linux (http://www.busybox.net/about.html) and combines numerous versions of many common UNIX utilities into a single small executable. The utilities in BusyBox generally have fewer options than their counterparts in GNU Linux, but behave similarly and in a perfectly adequate manner in most cases.

In the following chapters, I explain some programming samples that are intended to show the basic procedures. For working on these programming samples, an editor is sufficient, as Shell, Python and Lua scripts are executed interpretively.

At this point, a reference to the different standards for the line break in a text file should be noted. Using a script or a configuration file from the Windows environment can result in several problems when using Linux. How this can be dealt with easily is described in Section 5.1.

4.2.1   Shell Scripts

4.2.1.1   Boardinfo

Our used Linux provides a lot of information on the overall system. We can query this information by using shell commands, for example.

Listing 26 shows a shell script that queries information about the used CPU and the Linux version as well as the run time after the last boot process (uptime), the free memory of the processor (free) and of the flash card (df), and the connected USB devices (lsusb).

```sh
#!/bin/sh

echo "==============================="
echo "Arduino Yun Board Information"
echo "==============================="
echo
echo "--- CPU Info ---------------"
cat /proc/cpuinfo
echo
echo "---Linux Version ------------"
uname -a
echo
echo "--- Uptime ------------------"
uptime
echo
echo "--- Memory Usage ------------"
free -m
df -h echo
echo "--- USB --------------------"
lsusb -tv
```

Listing 26 Shell script *boardinfo.sh*

Figure 86 shows call and output of the shell script *boardinfo.sh*.

```
 mc [root@myYun]:~
root@myYun:~# ./boardinfo.sh
=====================================
Arduino Yun Board Information
=====================================

--- CPU Info ---------------
system type             : Atheros AR9330 rev 1
machine                 : Arduino Yun
processor               : 0
cpu model               : MIPS 24Kc V7.4
BogoMIPS                : 265.42
wait instruction        : yes
microsecond timers      : yes
tlb_entries             : 16
extra interrupt vector  : yes
hardware watchpoint     : yes, count: 4, address/irw mask: [0x0000, 0x0ff8, 0x0ff8, 0x0ff
8]
ASEs implemented        : mips16
shadow register sets    : 1
kscratch registers      : 0
core                    : 0
VCED exceptions         : not available
VCEI exceptions         : not available

---Linux Version -----------
Linux myYun 3.8.3 #8 Mon Aug 19 16:22:39 CEST 2013 mips GNU/Linux

--- Uptime ------------------
18:02:02 up  7:55,  load average: 0.21, 0.09, 0.06

--- Memory Usage -----------
                total        used        free      shared     buffers
Mem:            61132       40020       21112           0        4948
-/+ buffers:                35072       26060
Swap:               0           0           0
Filesystem             Size    Used Available Use% Mounted on
rootfs                 7.5M    6.6M    872.0K  89% /
/dev/root              7.0M    7.0M         0 100% /rom
tmpfs                 29.9M  472.0K     29.4M   2% /tmp
tmpfs                512.0K       0    512.0K   0% /dev
/dev/mtdblock3         7.5M    6.6M    872.0K  89% /overlay
overlayfs:/overlay     7.5M    6.6M    872.0K  89% /
/dev/sda1            243.9M  384.0K    243.5M   0% /mnt/sda1

--- USB --------------------
/:  Bus 01.Port 1: Dev 1, Class=root_hub, Driver=ehci-platform/1p, 480M
  |__ Port 1: Dev 2, If 0, Class=Hub, Driver=hub/4p, 480M
      |__ Port 4: Dev 3, If 0, Class=Mass Storage, Driver=usb-storage, 480M
root@myYun:~#
```

Figure 86 Call and output of the shell script *boardinfo.sh*

The data shown in Figure 86 indicate that our Arduino Yún has an Atheros AR9330 Yun rev. 1 processor. The difference between the Atheros AR9331 assigned to the Arduino Yún and the AR9330 given here, can no longer be traced on the Qualcomm Atheros website. A data sheet for the AR9331 can be found on the internet.

The data BogoMIPS: 265.42 is interesting but should not be misleading. BogoMIPS is a measure of CPU speed used in the Linux kernel. The value is determined at boot time. In a calibration loop, the NOP instruction of the CPU is measured to implement classic busy-wait delay loops in the nanosecond range within the kernel correctly.

The test introduced by Linus Torvalds shows in its name, which is derived from the English bogus (fake, apparently) and the unit millions of instructions per second (MIPS), that this is not a scientifically well-defined measure.

An often quoted definition is, "The number of million repetitions per second, which is a processor capable of doing absolutely nothing." BogoMIPS cannot be used to compare the performance between processors, but such statements are always found on the internet.

In addition to the Atheros AR9331, I could query this information from some other devices (Raspberry Pi, smartphones, and tablets). The results are shown in Table 7 below.

Device	Processor	Family	Bogo-MIPS
Arduino Yún	AtherosAR9331	MIPS24K	265.42
Raspberry Pi	BCM2835	ARM11	464.48
HTC Desire	ARMv7 Processor rev2 (v7I)	Cortex-A8	662.40
Archos70 Internet	ARMv7 Processor rev2 (v7I)	Cortex-A8	796.19
Samsung Galaxy S3	ARMv7 Processor rev0 (v7I)	SMDK4x12	1592.52
Banana Pi (912 MHz)	ARMv7 Processor rev4 (v7I)	AllWinner A20	1813.29
Samsung Galaxy Tab 10.1	ARMv7 Processor rev0 (v7I)	--	1982.85

Table 7 BogoMIPS of several Linux devices

In the Arduino Yún used here, a Linux kernel version 3.8.3 is installed on the Atheros AR9331.

The command `uptime` shows a run time of more than seven hours and 55 minutes after the last boot process. With `uptime`, we get information about the stability of a system. With `load average`, we get an indication of the average CPU load of the system. The average load in the last one, five or 15 minutes was 21, nine or six per cent here.

The next block lists the free and used memory of the system, as well as the buffer areas used by the kernel. The assignment of the SD

153

card is listed afterwards. The conclusion is the display of the devices connected via USB.

4.2.1.2   Synchronization of the system time

Most systems using OpenWRT as an operational system have no hardware clock. In most cases, a time reference cannot be waived and you would be looking for a suitable alternative.

An alternative is to enhance the system by a real-time clock (RTC). As an example, we consider the RTC module from Sparkfun (https://www.sparkfun.com/products/12708), but there are numerous other very similar modules on the market.

Figure 87 shows the RTC module with clock quartz and a DS1307 RTC device. On the rear is a mounted CR1225 lithium cell buffering the DS1307 RTC device.

Figure 87 RTC module

All software components can be downloaded from Sparkfun's website (https://github.com/sparkfun/RTC-Module).

Another alternative we get through an internet connection that is possible for our Arduino Yún.

The BusyBox on the Linux device provides us with *ntpd*, a network time protocol daemon that matches the system time with the time of a time server in the background. *Busybox-ntpd* must be configured in the file /etc/config/system. Per default, *ntpd* runs as client. The following arguments control *busybox-ntpd*:

```
# ntpd [-dnqNwl] [-S PROG] [-p PEER]...
```

Arguments:

-d	Verbose
-n	Do not daemonize
-q	Quit after clock is set
-N	Run at high priority
-w	Do not set time (only query peers), implies -n
-l	Run as server on port 123
-S PROG	Run PROG after stepping time, stratum change, and every 11 minutes
-p PEER	Obtain time from PEER (may be repeated)

According to Figure 88, you can convince yourself that *ntpd* is running here as a server on port 123 with the time synchronized in the background. When you call date, you can expect a time synchronized with a time server from the pool openwrt.pool.ntp.org.

```
192.168.1.4 - PuTTY
root@myYun:~# ps -w | grep ntpd
 1588 root      1504 S    /usr/sbin/ntpd -n -l -p 0.openwrt.pool.ntp.org -p 1.ope
nwrt.pool.ntp.org -p 2.openwrt.pool.ntp.org -p 3.o
31448 root      1496 S    grep ntpd
root@myYun:~# date
Sun Oct  5 04:48:47 CEST 2014
root@myYun:~#
```

Figure 88 *ntpd* running?

To increase the accuracy of time synchronization, it is advisable to work with time servers "up close" and to write them into the file /etc/config/system.

For Switzerland, this would be ch.pool.ntp.org and for Germany de.pool.ntp.org. In these zones, the digits 0, 1, 2 or 3 can be prefixed again (e.g. 0.de.pool.ntp.org). It should be noted that not all countries' time zones exist, or only a few time servers can be included in it.

To get a suitable time server for North America, the website http://www.pool.ntp.org/zone/north-america offers the right information.

However, time servers can be specified directly, too. The time server of the Physikalisch-Technische Bundesanstalt in Braunschweig (Germany) is a well-known address for Europe:

PTB Time Server 1 ptbtime1.ptb.de
PTB Time Server 2 ptbtime2.ptb.de
PTB Time Server 3 ptbtime3.ptb.de

I have made use of this option here and configured /etc/config/system accordingly (Figure 89).

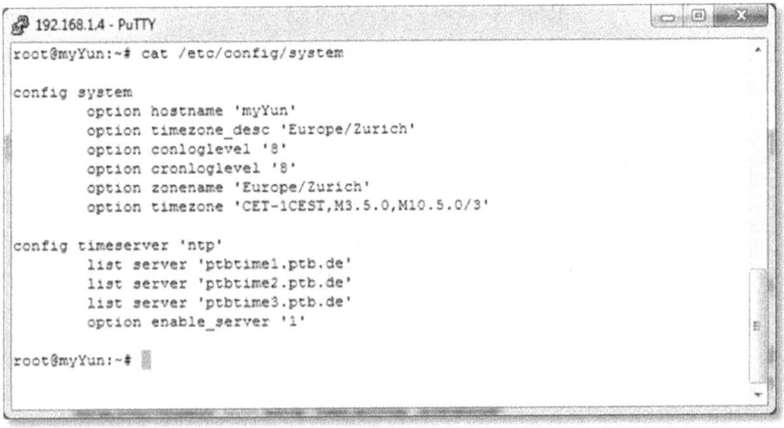

```
192.168.1.4 - PuTTY
root@myYun:~# cat /etc/config/system

config system
        option hostname 'myYun'
        option timezone_desc 'Europe/Zurich'
        option conloglevel '8'
        option cronloglevel '8'
        option zonename 'Europe/Zurich'
        option timezone 'CET-1CEST,M3.5.0,M10.5.0/3'

config timeserver 'ntp'
        list server 'ptbtime1.ptb.de'
        list server 'ptbtime2.ptb.de'
        list server 'ptbtime3.ptb.de'
        option enable_server '1'

root@myYun:~#
```

Figure 89 Configuration /etc/config/system

More information can be found at the URL http://www.pool.ntp.org/en/use.html.

4.2.1.3 Scaling with *bc*

In Chapter 4.1.3, we have already got to know the Basic Calculator *bc*. Based on a simple example, I want to show you how *bc* can be used for scaling values.

For our example, we start with a straight line equation

$$y = m * x + n$$

The value x should be multiplied with the factor m and the offset n is added afterward. This is a common task in the case of the scaling of the measured values.

The Basic Calculator *bc* can operate with a floating-point number without any trouble and should be used for scaling. In a shell script, we prepare the data for an operation by *bc*.

In the program sample, we start from the equation

y=2.5* x+ 1

and build the shell script *scale.sh* (Listing 27).

```
#!/bin/sh

echo "scale=6; $1 * 2.5 + 1" | bc
```
Listing 27 Shell script *scale.sh*

The command `echo` builds the equation and the input data for *bc*. A pipe (|) transfers these data to *bc* for calculation. In the argument of `echo`, we find `scale = 6` defining the decimal places for the result. The value x (argument when calling the script) is given by $1.

Figure 90 shows call and output of the shell script *scale.sh* after changing the permission to executable by the command `chmod +x scale.sh`. By `scale = 6` the number of decimal places was set to six. The last result is rounded to six decimal places.

The following article published in the German *Linux* magazine delivers information and hints about the usage of the Basic Calculators *bc* (http://www.pro-linux.de/artikel/2/909/der-basic-calculator-bc.html).

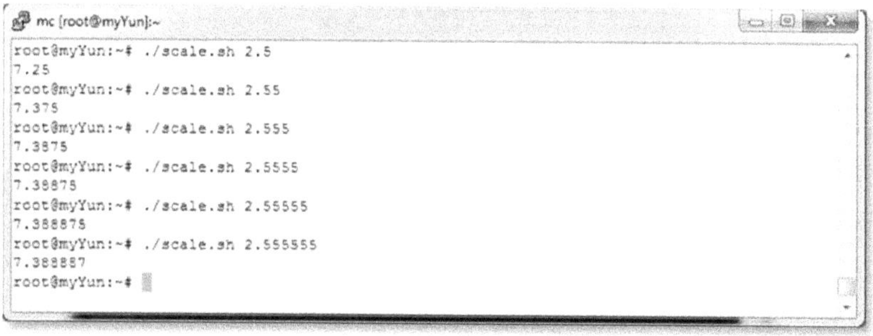

Figure 90 Call and output of the shell script *scale.sh*

4.2.1.4   Integrity Test of Files

Cryptographic hash algorithms like to be used for the test of integrity of files. Linux offers here in most distributions the MD5 (Message Digest Algorithm 5) or SHA1 (Secure Hash Algorithm 1). Both algorithms compute from any files a 128-bit or 160-bit hash value (checksum). Linino (OpenWRT) makes MD5 available.

A common use of these algorithms can be found in the file download from a file server on the Internet. The checksum of the original file is made available on the server and, after downloading the sum in question, can be calculated and compared against the checksum stored on the server. If the checksums are identical, then the downloaded file is intact and the download was successful.

Figure 91 shows the call of the MD5 algorithm to generate the checksum of the Shell *boardinfo.sh* (as an example) and saving this checksum in the file *boardinfo.md5*. The command `cat boardinfo.md5` outputs that value to the console. The command `md5sum -c boardinfo.md5` checks the generated checksum afterward.

It is also shown as a corrupt file that can be detected. In order to demonstrate a violation of the integrity of the file, a space is included into the file *boardinfo.sh*. The test of the checksum now points to an error. The calculated checksum of the corrupted file does not match the checksum stored in the file *boardinfo.md5*, which was generated from the intact file *boardinfo.sh*. The functionality of the shell scripts *boardinfo.sh* does not change because of the included space.

```
root@myYun:~# md5sum boardinfo.sh > boardinfo.md5
root@myYun:~# cat boardinfo.md5
f9e7a983aed7d7b75bb12ccdde4d665d  boardinfo.sh
root@myYun:~# md5sum -c boardinfo.md5
boardinfo.sh: OK
root@myYun:~# echo " " >> boardinfo.sh
root@myYun:~# md5sum -c boardinfo.md5
boardinfo.sh: FAILED
md5sum: WARNING: 1 of 1 computed checksums did NOT match
root@myYun:~#
```

Figure 91 Using *md5sum*

4.2.1.5   Cron Jobs

Cron is a daemon that allows certain operations to be performed automatically at defined times. These operations can be individual commands, shell scripts, programs, PHP and other scripts.

For example, backups that should be done daily or even hourly are normally performed as Cron jobs. A very good introduction to Cron jobs can be found in [10].

Let us consider the mechanism of Cron jobs using a simple example. The command `uptime` outputs the run time of the system since the last boot and system utilization, which will allow conclusions on the system behavior. With this command, a simple shell script *cronscript.sh* can be created, which writes the output of uptime in a logfile *cron.log* (Listing 28).

To append the current output to the file, the string ">>" must be used to redirect to the file. When you use ">" for redirection only, then the old content of the file is always overwritten and you have only the last entry available.

```
#! /bin/sh

uptime >> $HOME/cron.log
exit 0
```

Listing 28 Shell script *cronscript.sh*

After the script you just created is made executable, it can be called from the command line.

```
# chmod +x cronscript.sh
# ./cronscript.sh
```

We want to automate this process here, however, and run the script *cronscript.sh* every hour.

For this purpose, we use a table called Cron tab filed under /etc/crontabs/root. The individual Cron jobs are as defined and configured in this table. The table provides the timing and sequence of instructions to be executed per line.

We generate this file by the command

```
# touch/etc/crontabs/root
```

The actual Cron job definition is now in the following format:

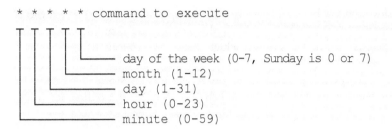

```
* * * * * command to execute
```

A comment line or a space terminates the Cron tab. Figure 92 shows the Cron tab created here. Further details can be found in the Cron man pages (Help on Cron).

Figure 92 Entry into the Cron tab

To start Cron at boot time, we prepare an initialization script by

touch/etc/init.d/S50cron

with the content according to Listing 29.

```
#!/bin/sh

# start crond
/etc/init.d/start
/etc/init.d/enable
```

Listing 29 Shell script *S50cron*

This script is made executable and run from the command line.

chmod +x /etc/init.d/S50cron
/etc/init.d/S50cron

Whether or not `crond` was started successfully, can now be checked by calling `logread` as shown in Figure 93.

```
mc [root@myYun]:~
root@myYun:~# logread | grep started
Oct  2 10:06:28 myYun cron.info crond[1416]: crond: crond (busybox 1.19.4) started, log l
evel 8
Oct  2 10:06:36 myYun daemon.info dnsmasq[1514]: started, version 2.62 cachesize 150
root@myYun:~#
```

Figure 93 Crond running?

If changes were made to the Cron tab, a restart should occur in the form:

```
# killall crond
# /etc/init.d/S50cron
```

4.2.1.6   Controlling a USB webcam

A webcam is, in most cases, a simple camera connected via USB to a computer. Defined events trigger these cameras to send still images or video streams. Additionally, text can be included into the image information.

Such USB webcams are offered today in a wide variety of types. Despite the large number of existing drivers, it can lead to unpleasant incompatibilities, especially because the information for an installation on Linux is often missing.

fswebcam is a simple webcam application, which can trigger such a webcam and download the image file. The images can be stored as PNG or JPG files (http://www.firestorm.cx/fswebcam/).

I have experimented with a USB webcam Logitech C270 connected to the USB port of Arduino Yún.

At first, I cleared the message buffer using

```
# sudo dmesg -c
```

to make the messages visible when connecting the USB webcam. Figure 94 shows the messages from installation after calling the commands `dmesg` and `lsusb`.

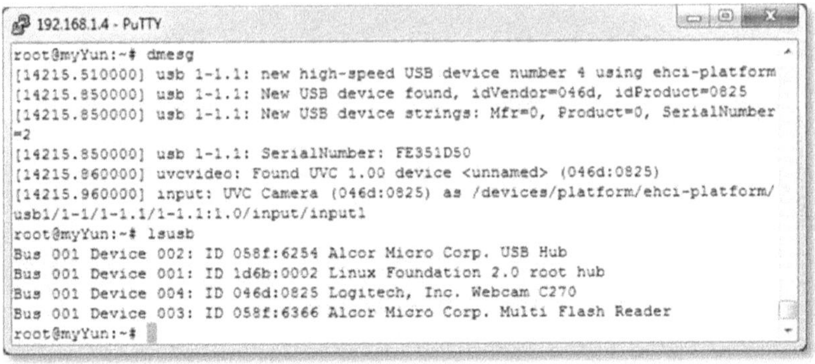

```
192.168.1.4 - PuTTY
root@myYun:~# dmesg
[14215.510000] usb 1-1.1: new high-speed USB device number 4 using ehci-platform
[14215.850000] usb 1-1.1: New USB device found, idVendor=046d, idProduct=0825
[14215.850000] usb 1-1.1: New USB device strings: Mfr=0, Product=0, SerialNumber
=2
[14215.850000] usb 1-1.1: SerialNumber: FE351D50
[14215.860000] uvcvideo: Found UVC 1.00 device <unnamed> (046d:0825)
[14215.960000] input: UVC Camera (046d:0825) as /devices/platform/ehci-platform/
usb1/1-1/1-1.1/1-1.1:1.0/input/input1
root@myYun:~# lsusb
Bus 001 Device 002: ID 058f:6254 Alcor Micro Corp. USB Hub
Bus 001 Device 001: ID 1d6b:0002 Linux Foundation 2.0 root hub
Bus 001 Device 004: ID 046d:0825 Logitech, Inc. Webcam C270
Bus 001 Device 003: ID 058f:6366 Alcor Micro Corp. Multi Flash Reader
root@myYun:~#
```

Figure 94 Installation of a USB webcam

The first command shows that a camera was found and the driver *UVC* was assigned. UVC stands for USB Video Class. It defines video streaming functionality on the Universal Serial Bus.

The second command delivers all USB components as connected. Device No. 004 is the connected Logitech webcam C270.

To test the installed USB webcam, we install the package *fswebcam*. A call of *fswebcam* triggers an image and saves it in the file *webcam-test.jpg*.

```
# opkg install fswebcam
# fswebcam -S1 -r1280x960 -d/dev/video0-
v/home/images/webcam_test.jpg
```

Figure 95 shows the call of the program *fswebcam* and the messages documenting the entire process of triggering, processing, and storage.

Figure 95 Triggering the webcam

To display the image captured from the Arduino Yún, it must be uploaded to the developer's PC that is connected to the network before it can be viewed by a picture viewer, such as Paint. Figure 96 shows such a snapshot from my window.

Figure 96 Snapshot

You can save the configuration data of the webcam in a separate configuration file to get fewer parameters for the call of *fswebcam*. Using an editor, we can generate the file *fswebcam.cfg* according to Figure 97.

Figure 97 Webcam configuration

The entries in the file *fswebcam.cfg* mean the following.

The first two lines address the connected webcam and will be used as default as well.

The parameter `skip 1` has the effect that the first frame is skipped and only the second is stored. This option is always helpful when the first frame has interferences or other similar issues.

The parameter `resolution` defines the resolution of the webcam.

The parameter `jpeg` influences the compression rate of the JPG file and the resulting quality of the image. For a value of 95, we get an image compressed with virtually no loss.

The parameter `save` defines the path and file name to store the image.

There are many other configuration parameters, but you must query `man fswebcam` to get this information. Figure 98 shows the call of program `fswebcam -c fswebcam.cfg` configured by a separate configuration file.

```
192.168.1.4 - PuTTY
root@myYun:~# fswebcam -c fswebcam.cfg

Trying source module v4l2...
/dev/video0 opened.

Skipping frame...
Capturing 1 frames...
Corrupt JPEG data: 2 extraneous bytes before marker 0xd2
Captured 2 frames in 0.03 seconds.

Setting output format to JPEG, quality 95
Unable to load font 'sans': libgd was not built with FreeType font support

Disabling the the banner.
Writing JPEG image to '/home/images/webcam_test.jpg'.
root@myYun:~#
```

Figure 98 Triggering the webcam with configuration file

If we trigger the webcam to get images periodically, then a reference to the recording date is of particular interest. I would like to include the date and time of recording into the file name here, for example.

The original image file that was stored as *webcam_test.jpg* gets a new file name in the form *webcam_test_YYYYMMDD-HHMM.jpg* (e.g. *webcam_test_20140208-1947.jpg*). The shell script *tr_image.sh* (Figure 99) outputs a message to the console followed by triggering and storing an image and then providing a copy of that file with the date and time of recording.

```
192.168.1.4 - PuTTY
root@myYun:~# cat tr_image.sh
#!/bin/sh

DATE_="$(date)"
echo -n "$DATE_"
echo " - Trigger image and save..."
fswebcam -c fswebcam.cfg
cp /home/images/webcam_test.jpg /home/images/webcam_test_$(date +%Y%m%d-%H%M).jp
g
root@myYun:~#
```

Figure 99 Shell script *tr_image.sh*

Figure 100 shows the call of the shell scripts *tr_image.sh* after it was taken as executable by `chmod +x tr_image.sh`.

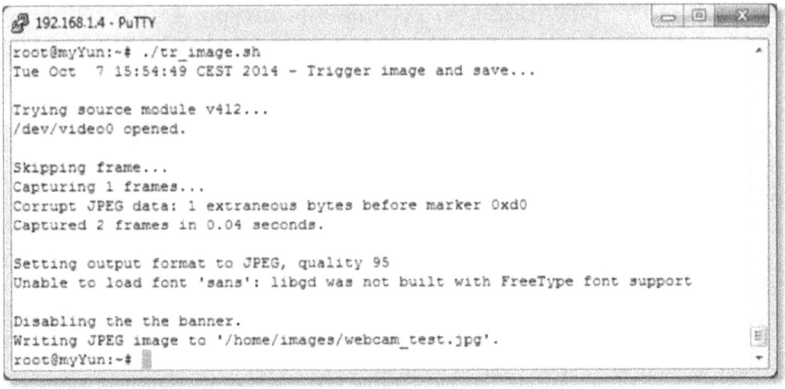

Figure 100 Dating of captured image files

The program *fswebcam* stores the actual image always with the file name *webcam_test.jpg*. The dated image files result through the copy process. Therefore, the file *webcam_test.jpg* is always identical to the last dated file. You can see this by examining the file sizes in Figure 101.

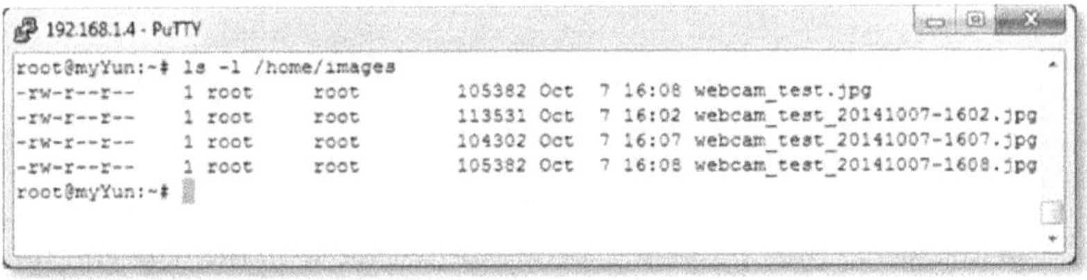

Figure 101 Dated image files

If you use the webcam for periodic shots, then fast extensive data may result that overwhelm the Arduino Yún memory. Here, a connected memory stick or practical unlimited cloud storage can help.

4.2.1.7 USB memory stick

The existing USB port can also be used for memory expansion with a memory stick. Since only one USB port is present on Arduino Yún, an intermediary USB hub helps when using a USB webcam and a USB memory stick.

We need the following software packages and it is possible that they may need to still be installed:

- kmod-usb-storage-kernel support for USB mass storage devices
- kmod-fs-<file_system>-kernel support for different file systems Common examples include kmod-fs-ext4, kmod-fs-hfs, kmod-fs-hfsplus, kmod-fs-ntfs, kmod-fs-reiserfs, and kmod-fs-vfat.
- block-mount-scripts used to mount and check block devices (file systems and swap) and hot plug capability (recognition when device is plugged in).

The installation is carried out as follows:

```
# opkg update
# opkg install kmod-usb-storage block-mountblock-
hotplug kmod-fs-ext4 kmod-fs-vfat kmod-nls-cp437
kmod-nls-iso8859-1
# mkdir -p /media/usb
# mount -t vfat /dev/sdb1 /media/usb
```

After the update, the required kernel modules are installed and the directory /media/usb is generated. Finally, the detected USB memory stick can be mounted.

Figure 102 shows that the inserted USB memory stick has been recognized as sdb1. Since we work here at the same time with an SD card, this was already assigned to sda1. The command ls/dev/sd* lists both memory extensions.

```
192.168.1.4 - PuTTY                                                    □ ▣ X

root@myYun:~# dmesg
[18352.490000] usb 1-1.1: new high-speed USB device number 5 using ehci-platfor
m
[18352.620000] usb 1-1.1: New USB device found, idVendor=08ec, idProduct=0008
[18352.620000] usb 1-1.1: New USB device strings: Mfr=1, Product=2, SerialNumbe
r=3
[18352.630000] usb 1-1.1: Product: Store 'n' Go
[18352.630000] usb 1-1.1: Manufacturer: Verbatim
[18352.630000] usb 1-1.1: SerialNumber: 0E80386151B0AC9B
[18352.640000] scsi1 : usb-storage 1-1.1:1.0
[18353.640000] scsi 1:0:0:0: Direct-Access     VBTM    Store 'n' Go    5.00 P
Q: 0 ANSI: 0 CCS
[18353.910000] sd 1:0:0:0: [sdb] 2013184 512-byte logical blocks: (1.03 GB/983
MiB)
[18353.920000] sd 1:0:0:0: [sdb] Write Protect is on
[18353.920000] sd 1:0:0:0: [sdb] Mode Sense: 23 00 80 00
[18353.920000] sd 1:0:0:0: [sdb] No Caching mode page present
[18353.930000] sd 1:0:0:0: [sdb] Assuming drive cache: write through
[18353.930000] sd 1:0:0:0: [sdb] No Caching mode page present
[18353.940000] sd 1:0:0:0: [sdb] Assuming drive cache: write through
[18353.940000]  sdb: sdb1
[18353.950000] sd 1:0:0:0: [sdb] No Caching mode page present
[18353.950000] sd 1:0:0:0: [sdb] Assuming drive cache: write through
[18353.950000] sd 1:0:0:0: [sdb] Attached SCSI removable disk
root@myYun:~# ls /dev/sd*
/dev/sda   /dev/sda1  /dev/sdb   /dev/sdb1
root@myYun:~#
```

Figure 102 Detection of a USB memory stick

Access to our USB memory stick is now via the path /media/usb as shown in Figure 103.

```
192.168.1.4 - PuTTY                                                    □ ▣ X

root@myYun:~# touch /media/usb/test.txt
root@myYun:~# echo "Das ist eine Zeile Text" > /media/usb/test.txt
root@myYun:~# echo "Das ist eine zweite Zeile Text" >> /media/usb/test.txt
root@myYun:~# cat /media/usb/test.txt
Das ist eine Zeile Text
Das ist eine zweite Zeile Text
root@myYun:~# cp /home/images/webcam* /media/usb/
root@myYun:~# ls /media/usb
test.txt                        webcam_test_20141007-1607.jpg
webcam_test.jpg                 webcam_test_20141007-1608.jpg
webcam_test_20141007-1602.jpg
root@myYun:~#
```

Figure 103 File access on memory stick

At first, I generated the file *test.txt* there and wrote two lines of text into this file. Thereafter, I copied webcam images from the folder /home/images/to /media/usb, and, finally, the command ls /media/usb lists all files in that folder.

If you want to remove the memory stick, then this should be done by `umount /media/usb`.

With these newly acquired storage options enabled through the USB memory stick, the shell script *tr_image.sh* can be extended (Listing 30). By calling the script in the form

```
# ./tr_image1.sh USB
```

the triggered image is copied in the folder /media/usb and, thus, no longer burdens the resources of Arduino Yún. If no parameter is passed on the command line, then the behavior of the script is unchanged.

```
#!/bin/sh

DATE_="$(date)" echo -n "$DATE_"
echo " - Trigger image and save..."
fswebcam -c fswebcam.cfg

case $1 in
  USB) echo "Save image on /media/usb/"
       cp /home/images/webcam_test.jpg
/media/usb/webcam_test_$(date +%Y%m%d-%H%M).jpg
    ;;
    *) echo -n "Save image on " pwd
       rm /home/images/webcam_test_*.jpg
       cp /home/images/webcam_test.jpg
/home/images/webcam_test_$(date +%Y%m%d-%H%M).jpg
esac
```

Listing 30 Shell script *tr_image1.sh*

4.2.2 Python

4.2.2.1 Pseudorandom Numbers

Random numbers are needed in various areas of computer science. For our concerns, the simulation of sensor signals and the testing algorithms are of most interest.

Almost every programming language has more or less good pseudorandom number generators. Since this method generates numbers that cannot be truly random numbers derived from a stochastic process, they are called pseudorandom numbers.

The Python script *RandomNumbers.py* (Listing 31) generates 100 pseudorandom numbers in a range from zero to 100 and stores these numbers in the CSV file (comma separated values) *random-nunbers.txt*.

In addition to the generation of a pseudorandom number through the statement r=random.randint(0,100), one can see here the file handling in Python.

To write an introductory text into the file, the file must be opened in w(rite) mode—e.g. it will be created. To write pseudorandom numbers into this file, it must later be opened in a(ppend) mode—e.g. the data will be appended to the content stored already. The format "%d, " ensures that after the number with a comma, a space follows.

```
#RandomNumbers.py

import random

random.random( )
print('Generate 100 Random Numbers in Range
(0,100) > randomnumbers.txt')
file = open('randomnumbers.txt', 'w')
file.write('100 Random Numbers in Range (0,
100)\n')
file.close()
#file = open('randomnumbers.txt').readlines()
#print file

for i in range(1,100):
r = random.randint(0, 100)
#   print ('%d ' % r)
file = open('randomnumbers.txt', 'a')
file.write('%d, ' % r)
file.close()

#file = open('randomnumbers.txt').readlines()
#print file
```

Listing 31 Python script *RandomNumbers.py*

Figure 104 shows call and output of the Python script *Random-Numbers.py*.

```
192.168.1.4 - PuTTY
root@myYun:~# python RandomNumbers.py
Generate 100 Random Numbers in Range (0,100) > randomnumbers.txt
root@myYun:~# cat randomnumbers.txt
100 Random Numbers in Range (0, 100)
57,44,69,9,25,87,74,94,40,17,27,99,75,15,5,54,18,99,51,19,11,31,41,73,88,91,33,5
,88,95,45,51,76,32,88,66,60,70,8,29,26,0,10,20,15,25,5,91,61,93,20,35,99,74,34,1
3,99,2,76,23,5,49,46,94,7,26,67,86,71,15,15,0,19,67,54,84,34,37,71,89,7,96,91,6,
root@myYun:~#
```

Figure 104 Pseudorandom numbers with Python script

In order to visualize the generated pseudorandom numbers, the text file can be opened on the developer's PC with a spreadsheet. Here, this is done using Microsoft Excel, as Figure 105 through Figure 107 show.

My Office package is in German, which is why you will find German text in the screen shots. Nevertheless, I believe that it will not cause much confusion.

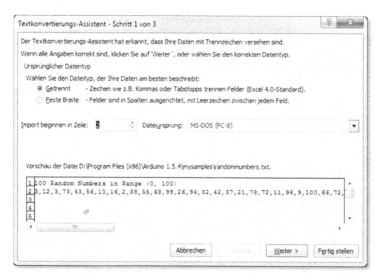

Figure 105 Text conversion for a CSV file using MS Excel (1)

Figure 106 Text conversion for a CSV file using MS Excel (2)

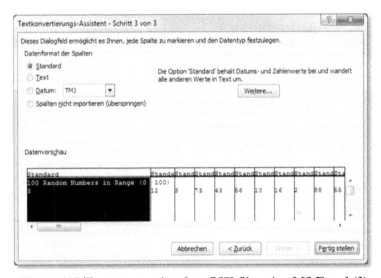

Figure 107 Text conversion for a CSV file using MS Excel (3)

Now, it only remains to visualize the graphical representation of pseudorandom numbers, which is shown in Figure 108.

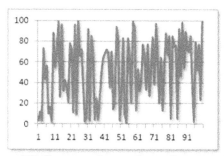

Figure 108 Generated pseudorandom numbers

4.2.2.2   Image Processing

The Python Imaging Library (PIL) is a free library for Python and offers support for the image processing of numerous image data formats.

The Python Imaging Library supports many standard methods for image processing. Wikipedia lists

- per-pixel manipulations
- masking and transparency handling
- image filtering, such as blurring, contouring, smoothing, or edge finding
- image enhancing, such as sharpening, adjusting brightness, contrast or color
- adding text to images and much more.

Supported are several image data formats, such as PPM, PNG, JPEG, GIF, TIFF and BMP. *The Python Imaging Library Handbook* (http://effbot.org/imagingbook/) explains the usage of the library in detail.

The PIL is installed as a package by the command:

```
# opkg install python-imaging-library
```

The following example illustrates the usage of PIL in the Python interpreter (Figure 109).

```
192.168.1.4 - PuTTY
root@myYun:~# python
Python 2.7.3 (default, Aug  8 2013, 22:36:42)
[GCC 4.6.4 20121210 (prerelease)] on linux2
Type "help", "copyright", "credits" or "license" for more information.
>>> from PIL import Image
>>> myImage = Image.open("ArduinoYun.jpg")
>>> myImage.rotate(90).save("ArduinoYun_90.jpg")
>>> ^C
KeyboardInterrupt
>>>
```

Figure 109 RotationArduinoYun.jpg

At first, the image module is imported from the PIL before the image file *ArduinoYun.jpg* can be opened. The method `rotate()` rotates the content of an image file by the specified angle counter-clockwise. This file is finally saved under the name *ArduinoYun_90.jpg*. Figure 110 shows the original image file and Figure 111 shows the result of the rotation of the image content.

**Figure 110
ArduinoYun.jpg**

**Figure 111
ArduinoYun_90.jpg**

This very basic example illustrates how easily complex tasks can be solved using appropriate libraries.

4.2.3   Lua

4.2.3.1   Data Functions

Listing 32 presents the source code of the Lua script *date.lua* and should demonstrate the possibility of formatted output.

Date and time were queried by the operating system call `os.date()` and formatted assigned to the variables `date` and

174

time. The function io.write() outputs the composite result string to the console.

```
-----------------------------------------------
-- Reads Date & Time from Linino (Atheros AR9331)
-----------------------------------------------
io.write("Date & Time from Linino:\n")
date = os.date("%Y-%m-%d")
time = os.date("%X")
io.write("Today is "..date.." "..time.."\n")
```

Listing32 Lua script *date.lua*

Figure 112 shows the call and output of the Lua script *date.lua*.

Figure 112 Call and output of Lua script *date.lua*

4.2.3.2 WiFi Info

With *pretty-wifi-info.lua*, our Linino system offers a Lua script that displays all WiFi-relevant data (Listing 33).

Controlled by the function collect_wifi_info(), the functions get_basic_net_info() and get_wifi_info() collect all data from the actual network. A number of print() instructions provides the output of the collected properties then. Figure 113 shows the call and output of the Lua script *pretty-wifi-info.lua* at the end.

```
#!/usr/bin/lua

local function get_basic_net_info(network, iface,
accumulator)
  local net = network:get_network(iface)
  local device = net and net:get_interface()

  if device then
```

```lua
    accumulator["uptime"] = net:uptime()
    accumulator["iface"] = device:name()
    accumulator["mac"] = device:mac()
    accumulator["rx_bytes"] = device:rx_bytes()
    accumulator["tx_bytes"] = device:tx_bytes()
    accumulator["ipaddrs"] = {}

    for _, ipaddr in ipairs(device:ipaddrs()) do
      accumulator.ipaddrs[#accumulator.ipaddrs + 1] = {
        addr = ipaddr:host():string(),
        netmask = ipaddr:mask():string()
      }
    end
  end
end

local function get_wifi_info(network, iface, accu-
mulator)
  local net = network:get_wifinet(iface)

  if net then
    local dev = net:get_device()
    if dev then
      accumulator["mode"] = net:active_mode()
      accumulator["ssid"] = net:active_ssid()
      accumulator["encryption"] =
net:active_encryption()
      accumulator["quality"] =
net:signal_percent()
    end
  end
end

local function collect_wifi_info()
  local network = re-
quire"luci.model.network".init()
  local accumulator = {}
  get_basic_net_info(network, "lan", accumulator)
  get_wifi_info(network, "wlan0", accumulator)
  return accumulator
end

local info = collect_wifi_info()

print("Current WiFi configuration")
```

```lua
if info.ssid then
  print("SSID: " .. info.ssid)
end
if info.mode then
  print("Mode: " .. info.mode)
end
if info.quality then
  print("Signal: " .. info.quality .. "%")
end
if info.encryption then
  print("Encryption method: " .. info.encryption)
end
if info.iface then
  print("Interface name: " .. info.iface)
end
if info.uptime then
  print("Active for: " .. math.floor(info.uptime /
60) .. " minutes")
end
if #info.ipaddrs > 0 then
  print("IP address: " .. info.ipaddrs[1].addr ..
"/" .. info.ipaddrs[1].netmask)
end
if info.mac then
  print("MAC address: " .. info.mac)
end
if info.rx_bytes and info.tx_bytes then
  print("RX/TX: " .. math.floor(info.rx_bytes /
1024) .. "/" .. math.floor(info.tx_bytes / 1024)
.. " KBs")
end
```

Listing 33 Lua script *pretty-wifi-info.lua*

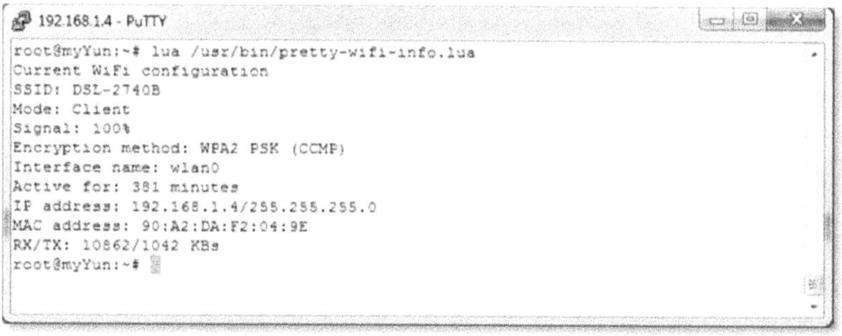

Figure 113 Call and output of *pretty-wifi-info.lua*

The Arduino Yún uses a chip antenna; hence, the signal strength is affected by external influences, such as distance to the router, shielding an added Arduino shield or housing, etc.

For the Dragino Yún shield, an external antenna can be used. For this purpose, an i-pex connector is on board allowing the necessary flexibility.

In my tests with the Dragino Yún shield, I was able to increase the signal strength of between 40 and 60 per cent to 100 per cent by connecting the supplied antenna. This is only a qualitative indication which, however, already shows the effect of this simple antenna.

Figure 114 shows the Dragino Yún shield with an external WiFi antenna attached.

Figure 114 Dragino Yún shield with external WiFi antenna

4.2.4   C

In the previous chapters, we have seen several examples that had been created as a shell, Lua or Python script. On most Linux devices one also has the GNU C compiler *gcc* available to compile application programs directly on the target.

Here, under Linino (OpenWRT), this is not the case. Hence, it takes a suitably equipped developer's PC to compile a C/C++ source code for our target. Here, one should refer to the WordPress page [12] describing cross-compilation for OpenWRT; otherwise, the scope of these introductory considerations would burst.

5 Appendix

The following chapters present some additional information. Their arrangement with regard to the rest of the text was not clear, but the information itself is sometimes helpful.

5.1 Line Break

There are several standards for coding a line break in a text file:

OS Class	Combination of Characters	ASCII Representation			ESC
		decimal	octal	hex	
Unix, Linux, Android, MacOS X, AmigaOS, BSD, etc.	LF	10	012	0x0A	\n
Windows, DOS, OS/2, CP/M, TOS(Atari)	CRLF	1310	015012	0x0D0x0A	\r\n
MacOS up to version 9, Apple II,C64	CR	13	015	0x0D	\r

Difficulties occur especially if you want to use a text file from Windows under Linux, for example. One example should clarify this.

Through a search with my Windows machine, I found on the web a graphical equivalent to the command df. I transferred this shell script *gdf.sh* to the Arduino Yún and opened it in the editor.

Figure 115 shows that each line ends with ^M. When calling this script, errors will occur. If you open this text file using a hex editor, then you will recognize immediately ^M is the Windows line break CRLF(\r\n).

To change the line break and make it Linux compliant, most Linux distributions contain the program *dos2unix*. In the Linino (OpenWRT) distribution available here, I could not find it. Hence, it was necessary to remove the character \r through existing means. The following command can assume that:

```
# cat gdf.sh | tr -d '\r' > gdf
```

Now, the first line must be adjusted because the Bash must be used since it is a more powerful shell. Afterward, the file can be saved as *gdf.sh*.

After making this shell script executable by

```
# chmod +x gdf.sh
```

it may finally be started as shown in Figure 116.

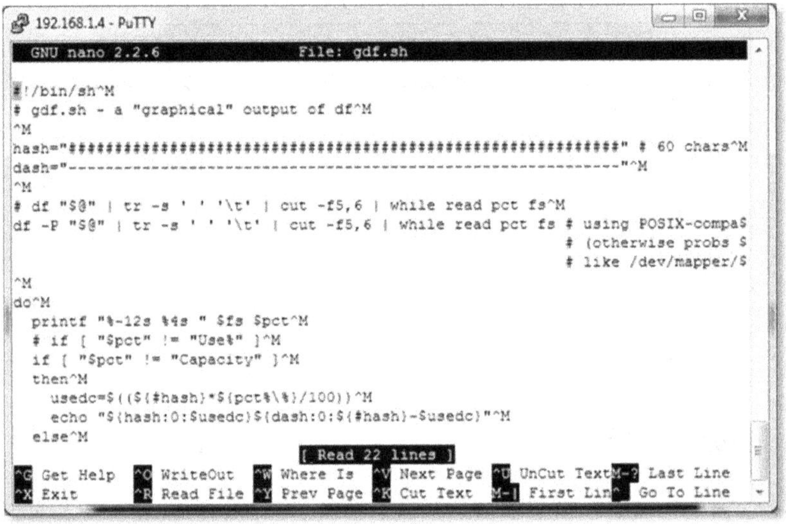

Figure 115 Shell script *gdf.sh* in editor

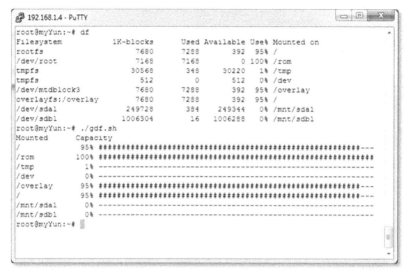

```
root@myYun:~# df
Filesystem            1K-blocks      Used Available Use% Mounted on
rootfs                     7680      7288       392  95% /
/dev/root                  7168      7168         0 100% /rom
tmpfs                     30568       348     30220   1% /tmp
tmpfs                       512         0       512   0% /dev
/dev/mtdblock3             7680      7288       392  95% /overlay
overlayfs:/overlay         7680      7288       392  95% /
/dev/sda1                249728       384    249344   0% /mnt/sda1
/dev/sdb1               1006304        16   1006288   0% /mnt/sdb1
root@myYun:~# ./gdf.sh
Mounted       Capacity
/                  95% ###################################################------
/rom              100% ###########################################################
/tmp                1% -----------------------------------------------------------
/dev                0% -----------------------------------------------------------
/overlay           95% ###################################################------
/                  95% ###################################################------
/mnt/sda1           0% -----------------------------------------------------------
/mnt/sdb1           0% -----------------------------------------------------------
root@myYun:~#
```

Figure 116 Call of df and *gdf.sh*

5.2 Access Data

In this chapter, the various access data can be recorded centrally. The sometimes seemingly hopeless search for yellow stickers or other shelves can be avoided.

ARDUINO YÚN See Chapter 2.7	Arduino Yún configuration Hostname: myYun (used here) Login: root (used here) Password: _____	p. 28
www.putty.org	Hostname: 192.168.x.y Login: root Password: _____	p. 132
http://winscp.net/eng/	Hostname: 192.168.x.y Login: root Password:_____	p. 135
arviXe owncloud http://www.arvixe.com/	FTP Information Host: .owncloud.arvixe.com FTP Username: . FTP Password:_	p. 148
Google www.google.com	email: _____ Password:_____	p. 104
Temboo https://temboo.com/	email: _____ Password:_____	p. 101
twilio CLOUD COMMUNICATIONS https://www.twilio.com/	email: _____ Password:_____	p. 126

5.3 Python Packages

When using Python, it is important to know which packages (modules, libraries) are available. The command

```
# opkg list | grep python > python_packages
```

lists all available Python packages and stores this list in the file *python_packages*. Some of the packages are yet to be installed, as was also demonstrated in Chapter 4.2.2.2 for the Python Image Library.

Here is a list of all Python packages available in the used version of Linino (OpenWRT). The used packages are marked with a gray background here:

```
ipython - 0.8.2-1 - An enhanced interactive Py-
thon shell from the SciPy project logilab-astng -
0.17.2-1 - The aim of this module is to provide a
common base repre- sentation of python source
code for projects such as pychecker, pyreverse,
pylint... logilab-common - 0.29.1-1 - a bunch of
modules providing low level functionnalities
shared among some python projects devel
pyserial - 2.4-1 - serial port python bindings
python - 2.7.3-2 - Python is a dynamic object-
oriented programming language that can beused for
many kinds of software development. It offers
strong support for integration with other lan-
guages and tools, comes with extensive standard
libraries, and can be learned in a few days. Many
Python programmers report substantial productivi-
ty gains and feel the language encourages the de-
velopment of higher quality, more maintainable
code.
. This package contains the full Python install.
python-bluez - 0.13-1 - Python wrapper for the
BlueZ Bluetooth stack python-bzip2 - 2.7.3-2 -
Python support for Bzip2
python-cjson - 1.0.5-1 - Fast JSON encod-
er/decoder for Python
python-crypto - 2.6-1 - A collection of both se-
cure hash functions (such as MD5 and
```

SHA), and various encryption algorithms (AES, DES, IDEA, RSA, ElGamal, etc.). python-curl - 7.19.0-1 - Python module interface to the cURL library.
python-cwiid - 0.6.00-2 - Python bindings for the cwiid libs
python-django - 1.3.1-1 - Django is a high-level Python Web framework that encourages rapid development and clean, pragmatic design.
python-doc - 2.7.3-2 - Python interactive documentation
python-eeml - 20111202-1 - A python package for generating eeml documents.
python-egenix-mx - 2.0.6-1 - This package contains a set of base packages from Egenix required by other python packages.
python-event - 0.3-1 - Python interface to libevent python-expat - 2.7.3-2 - Python support for expat
python-flup - 1.0.2-1 - Random assortment of WSGI servers python-gdbm - 2.7.3-2 - Python support for gdbm
python-gobject - 2.21.5-1 - GLib bindings for python python-gzip - 2.7.3-2 - Python support for gzip
python-ifconfig - 0.1-2 - Display network interface status.
python-imaging-library - 1.1.7-2 - The Python Imaging Library adds image processing capabilities to your Python interpreter. . This library provides extensive file format support, an efficient internal representation, and fairly powerful image processing capabilities. The core image library is designed for fast access to data stored in a few basic pixel formats. It should provide a solid foundation for a general image processing tool.
python-json - 3_4-1 - json-py
python-kid - 0.9.6-1 - Kid is a simple template language for XML based vocabularies written in Python.
python-mimms - 3.2.1-1 - mimms is an mms (e.g. mms://) stream downloader
python-mini - 2.7.3-2 - Python is a dynamic object-oriented programming language that can be

used for many kinds of software development. It offers strong support for inte- gration with other languages and tools, comes with extensive standard libraries, and can be learned in a few days. Many Python programmers report substantial productivity gains and feel the language encourages the development of higher quality, more maintainable code. . This package contains only a minimal Python install.
python-mysql - 1.2.2-1 - MySQLdb is an thread-compatible interface to the popular MySQL database server that provides the Python database API. python-ncurses - 2.7.3-2 - Python support for readline python-openssl - 2.7.3-2 - Python support for OpenSSL python-pcap - 1.1-1 - Python interface to lipcap
python-psycopg - 1.1.21-1 - This package contains is a PostgreSQL database adapter for the Python programming language.
python-pydaemon - 0.2.3-1 - Turn python scripts into Unix daemons
python-pyosc - 0.3.5b-5294-1 - A simple Open-SoundControl implementation in pure Python python-rsfile - 1.1-1 - RockSolidTools' file I/O implementation
python-shutil - 2.7.3-2 - Python support for shutil python-sip - 4.12.1-1 - Python SIP
python-sqlite - 2.3.5-1 - This package contains an SQLite database adapter for the Python programming language.
python-sqlite3 - 2.7.3-2 - Python support for sqlite3 python-webpy - 0.37-2 - python-webpy
python-xapian - 1.2.8-1 - xapian python bindings
python-yapsnmp - 0.7.8-1 - This package contains a Python SNMP module based on the net- snmp (formerly known as ucd-snmp) library. It's composed of a low level interface to the library, created using SWIG, and a higher level python module removing all the com- plexity out of dealing with SNMP.
python2-chardet - 2.0.1-1 - Character encoding auto-detection in Python. pyusb - 0.4.2-1 - usb port python bindings
pyyaml - 3.08-1 - yaml python bindings

5.4 Arduino Yún Case

The English company SB Components offers a case specially developed for the Arduino Yún (http://stores.ebay.co.uk/sbcomponentsltd/).

The two-piece injection molded housing protects the Arduino Yún, but still allows access to all connectors of the board. The housing includes so-called light pipes for LEDs located on the board and allows access to the reset button. Figure 117 shows a case containing the Arduino Yún.

Figure 117 Arduino Yún case developed by SB Components (UK)

6 References and Links

[1]   Mark Weiser
        The Computer for the 21st Century
        http://www.ubiq.com/hypertext/weiser/SciAmDraft3.html

[2]   Why Google Choosing Arduino Matters and Is This the End
        of "Made for iPod"(TM)?
        Posted by Phillip Torrone, May 12, 2011
        blog.makezine.com/archive/2011/05/why-google-
        choosing-arduino-matters-and-the-end-of-made-for-ipod-
        tm.html

[3]   Thomas Brühlmann
        Arduino Praxiseinstieg: Behandelt Arduino1.0
        ISBN978-3-8266-9116-4 (Print);
        ISBN978-3-8266-8342-8 (PDF)

[4]   Claus Kühnel
        Arduino: Hard- und Software Open Source Plattform
        ISBN978-3907857-16-8 (Print);
        ISBN978-3-8448-9134-8 (eBook)

[5]   ATmega16U4/32U4 Preliminary
        (file size: 6.22MB, 433pages, revision G; updated: 02/2014)
        http://www.atmel.com/Images/Atmel-7766-8-bit-AVR-
        ATmega16U4-32U4_%20Datasheet.pdf

[6]   Internal   Temperature   Sensor—Using   the   Internal
        Temperature Sensor of the AVR Chip
        http://playground.arduino.cc/Main/InternalTemperatureSen
        sor

[7]   AVR122: Calibration of the AVR's Internal Temperature
        Reference
        http://www.atmel.com/Images/doc8108.pdf

[8]   cURL mit 6 praktischen Beispielen erklärt
        http://blog.thomas-falkner.de/2011/01/25/curl-mit-6-
        praktischen-beispielen-erklaert/

[9]   15 Practical Linux cURL Command Examples
        (cURL Download Examples)
        http://www.thegeekstuff.com/2012/04/curl-examples/

[10]   Crontab Tutorial und Syntax:
        Cronjobs unter Linux einrichten und verstehen
        http://stetix.de/cronjob-linux-tutorial-und-crontab-
        syntax.html

[11]   OpenWRT—Linux Distribution for Embedded Devices
        https://openwrt.org/

[12]   Writing and Compiling a Simple Program for OpenWRT
        http://manoftoday.wordpress.com/2007/10/11/writing-
        and-compiling-a-simple-program-for-openwrt/

Related Links:

Information and Source Code
http://sourceforge.net/projects/arduinoynsnippets/

Linux Wiki
https://openwrt.org/
http://de.linwiki.org/wiki/Hauptseite
http://wiki.ubuntuusers.de/Startseite
http://de.wikibooks.org/wiki/Linux-Kompendium
https://wiki.archlinux.de/
http://www.linux-magazin.de/
http://www.linux-fuer-alle.de/

7 Index

8 List of Figures

Notes

Your opinion or findings may also be of benefit to others.

Here, you will find space to record your notes, additions and hints.

You can send us appropriate instructions via the author's website (http://www.ckuehnel.ch). Please use this opportunity in the interest of the entire readership.